Title Page - Volume Two

An Inspired & Connected Leadership

A Collection of Life Examples Explored Through Branding

Volume Two, of Two

by

Randy Zeyen

SpinMonkeys Publishing Spyndicate

Volume Two
Introduction

"We all have room for improvement. Thankfully for me, this world is really, really big." - Randy Zeyen

If you read Volume One, then you already know how much I love to talk about branding. I am fascinated by the topic. I know that identifying with customers, connecting with them in a real way, and letting them know that you can relate to them on some intimate level, is essential to becoming successful in business.

This is the second volume of my thoughts focused upon the art of personal connecting, which is the basis for branding. As with the first, this book isn't a paint-by-numbers marketing guide either, but more of a collection of my thoughts you might use to inspire future discussions.

Humans are amazingly complex, unique and abstract beings, capable of accomplishing very incredible things.

We are a combination of:

    Physical – material and tangible

    Spiritual – abstract and transcendent

    Emotional – passionate and malleable

Power brands and great leaders make it primary to understand this, to utilize its power, and to protect the fluidity of this process. Once uncovered, they seek to foster ways to merge these three human realms, and help consumers to learn even more about themselves. This empowers those of us in business, to connect with them on even deeper spiritual and emotional levels.

As I've said many times, this message is personal to me. I just love to connect.

Volume Two
Chapters

chapter		pg
1	How to Become (a) Popular (Brand)	1
2	Your Smile is Your Logo	27
3	You Are a Styrofoam Cup	35
4	Pushing and Pulling	45
5	Inspiration and Realignment	59
6	Pace Maker or Pace Setter	79
7	Failure is a Cruel Word	95
8	Why Some Brands Lack Maturity	107
9	What Star Trek Can Teach Us	121
10	Feeling is Not Believing	143
11	Social Branding and Privacy	153
12	Your Artsy-Fartsy Creatives Deserve Better	171
13	The Hungry and the Foolish	205
14	Why You Should Hire a Monkey	223
15	Stay Thirsty, My Friends	233

Chapter One

How to Become (a) Popular (Brand)

Have you ever wanted to be popular?

Quite a few of us have had secret aspirations to become popular at one time in their life. Nearly all of us want to fit in, to be a significant part of some social group, or to become financially comfortable, or famous. In fact, this is what the word pop*ular means, to easily fit into a pop*ulation.

There are some of us who will gamble or play the lottery in hopes of prospering beyond their wildest dreams. Others, will put years of practice into tediously perfecting a special skill. Then again, some will do this by earning personal achievements or business accolades – others through deep friendships, spiritual journeys, or exclusive club memberships. We all want to be accepted, or yearn to be loved in a meaningful way, and we believe that being popular is one way of achieving this goal.

There's nothing wrong in being well liked by others, to be outlandishly prosperous, to possess extraordinary skills, or world renown fame…or all of them combined! But ultimately, what most of us truly desire, is to identify our singularly distinct aspiration in life; to feel secure in the knowledge of our unique purpose for being born on this earth — to know how we fit in to the big picture of life on earth.

Not everyone will find their way to realizing this ambition, or will be aware how to achieve it, but I will do my best here to shine a tiny light on why it appears to elude many.

You might want to know right now, that I see, and am about to share, three distinct and differing types of popularity. Each of them have its own individual significances and life expectations that will change the way you live your life, and love your work.

Two Types of Popularity

ANTI-SOCIAL POPULARITY
There are some celebrated super-achievers who are recluse and introspective, having achieved unwanted notoriety. Wealthy entrepreneur Howard Hughes, Greta Garbo, mega-rocker David Bowie, copper heiress Huguette Clark, and genius comic Johnny Carson were all famous, but are also solitary celebrity loners. They may have been admired and respected, and yet privately, they

led an extremely exclusive lifestyle. We have a number of famous recluses today that we could name. Fully aware of how they fit in, they feverishly recoil from the notability that accompanies them. They are a very different celebrity breed from the ordinary.

In this individual, an inward reflection will always supersede personal vanity or surface jubilance.

SOCIAL POPULARITY

There is also the conventional genre of "popular". In them, whose deep desire is to be separately distinguished from others, they love to be seen openly in public. Extroverts, they're always the first in line, the loudest in school, and in the front pew in church. Some become statuesque, blustery individuals whose sole desire in life is to shine brighter than everyone else, or strong leaders who speak in a way that make us feel safe. A small number of these become intellectual oracles able to see into the future, further than we ourselves. There are social media icons, super celebs, or vacuous brand luminaries.

In this peculiar type, the goal is clear – to be seen, to win, and to be seen as winning.

As I mentioned at the beginning of the chapter, there are three types of popularity, and I've just mentioned two of them. But, there is one more type that I haven't introduced yet and I've saved it for last for a good reason. It's different from the other two. Very different. In fact, this type of Popularity is so dissimilar, it really should be identified by another label entirely. If I had the time to come up with a better word for it I would, but instead, and for brevity reasons, I'm just going to refer to this last type as "Popularity," and the other two (mentioned above) as "Celebrity". You'll see why later.

Popularity is not Celebrity

There really is a difference between Popularity and Celebrity. They're not the same thing at all, although It is completely understandable how, at first, one might be confused with the other.

Pulitzer Prize author John Updike once said, *"Celebrity is a mask that eats into the face."* This quote may sound visually unpleasant. Reading it may temporarily leave a psychological mark behind, but still, I love this quote. To be sure, being celebrated can change a person, but this is not all that Updike is communicating. He's explaining how it can deconstruct a person, and their goals too. Celebrity has the nasty potential to evolve a well-intentioned person into an unrecognizable creation. Sadly for those inflicted, after a period of time, they wouldn't even be able to recognize themselves in a crowded room.

We've all been exposed to individuals like this. Most of us can identify them instinctively. Those free spirits that seem to be made of Teflon®. Their self-centered character traits will eventually give their true natures away.

Both of these two types may be seen by people as popular, but neither really are Popular, in the strict literal sense. They don't fit in. They are focused purely upon self.

Anti-Social Popularity persons may outwardly be loners, but their focus is upon the all importance self, by hiding away. They desire the consideration and attention of others, only to give the impression that they reject it outwardly. They hoard their popularity to benefit themselves alone.

Social Popularity comes across visually as contrary to the Anti-Social type, by placing self wherever the light is the brightest. And, wherever they stand, the sun seems to follow them. Ask them and they'll tell you so. All the admiration they receive, they bank for future leverage.

Both Anti-Social and Social Popularity are actually Celebrity, which are forms of ego idolatry – loving self above all else, excluding others, and any original underlying objective. Here, we've confused popularity with celebrity.

We should never forget that status (or stardom) has a tendency over time, to tarnish and lose its shine. Once the surface radiance has gone (youth, money, beauty, power), if there is no subcutaneous insight, all of the promise, the gleaming aspirations, will dematerialize too. Please understand me - I'm not subscribing that popularity is a bad thing. Not at all. Celebrity, on the other hand, will have a tendency to lose its luster, and its objective, over time. This we should avoid.

Scottish rebel Sir William Wallace was, in his time, considered popular…and yet, it was his ideology, his love for country over self, and not his distinctive personage that people were drawn to. Doing the right thing, at the right time, and for the right reasons, can withstand the wear-and-tear of time. Natural law suggests that patina will always appear. You can dismiss it is happening, but it is undeniable. You will be deeply disappointed and need to plan for this. Once the oxidation is removed, only the infrastructure and the foundation will be revealed. Hopefully you've spent plenty of effort utilizing any popularity you've collected to be in tune, to harmonize with the society in which you live.

Popularity Can Be a Good Goal

Corporate and personal brands desire to become popular too, thinking it is the way to profits and financial success. And, they're sold this imperative by robust and aggressive, or by pop-centered branding groups. Here is what people repeat to themselves, *"Any news, is good news. It means you're the center of attention."* Yes, I've heard this message quoted much to often. Unfortunately, the real truth is (in business) bad news is never good at all, no matter what they tell you. Don't believe them. Bad news may bring Celebrity, but it will usually only bring good news for someone else. I'm not unenlightened by the concept that prestige will undoubtedly equate to some type of short-term financial success. I understand this tactic may have an impact…but it will not last, and it cannot be sustained.

Gorilla marketers, blitzkrieg branding, and social promotion gurus may be able to temporarily shake the walls of your business – meanwhile, they can get it very, very wrong. They really do miss the point. After all, the goal of connecting is not about turning mesmerized heads, it is about raising enlightened eyebrows.

They may be able to create some form of product or brand awareness, but concealed deep within the messages will be negative information. As with individuals, brands can crave attention for the wrong reasons. If the primary desire is to create wealth, fame, landscape or power, to what end? What is the eventual payoff you'd expect? Sadly, many companies will sacrifice long-term success for short-term profitability. And yet, even in today's whirlwind of social media, and overnight notoriety, I believe it is very possible to become well-liked and marketable by being true to self, inclusive of others, and involved in your community.

You won't have to achieve three million clicks online, construct a grand hotel in every major city, or a freeway with your name posted on it. You won't need to bullwinkle CNN with a false news story to achieve fame, and become one of those influential and historical, maverick icons. No need to try that hard, you'll already be Popular.

PRO-SOCIAL POPULARITY

These simple steps will lead you to personally (or corporately) become truly popular.

A. Be Yourself

Yes, you've heard this saying before…*"just be yourself"*.

If only it were this easy, but here's a good way to begin. Evaluate why you want to become popular.

As a youth, I was impressed by the actor, David Janssen. From 1963 to 1967, I'd comb my hair just like Dr. Richard Kimble on the television show "The Fugitive". Later on, in the early 70's, the Beatles, the Beach Boys and the Rolling Stones would grab my attention, and my personal style. Like most people, I've morphed throughout the decades into my personage today. And, although my wife wishes I were sometimes a little less so sometimes…I'm comfortable. I don't dress for success. I dress for me.

Initially, it is essential to know "why" you are. Notice I didn't say, "who" you are, but "why". You may think I'm trying to be obscure and profound, but I assure you, I'm not. As I see it, if I am going to give you procedural steps, I should begin at the genesis…the why. Every thing, everywhere begins with "why". People do things for reasons. The earth quakes and ocean waves go tidal because something else happened somewhere else first. The earth, it's elements, your company and you, are only a product of the past. So, it is key to realize that, who you are, will become evident pretty quickly, once you know why you exist, and your purpose in the world.

Musicians, Bjork, Lady Gaga, Marilyn Manson, and Katy Perry have built careers on their personal style. Apple's Steve Jobs had a very simple signature look of blue jeans, black mock turtleneck and New Balance® sneakers. Albert Einstein stuck to one simple grey suit.

Famous people and power-brand companies are known for a consistent style because:

1) it has become their brand identity (or how they are distinctively identified)…and

2) it separates how they appear (from what they've accomplished)

Honesty is the cornerstone. The common thread that separates popular people or brands from celebrity, comes down to one simple thing — how they execute integrity.

So, before you dedicate time, effort, and/or resources to making yourself popular, take a moment to evaluate your desire – your prime directive. Never alter your round brand to fit in a square space, or coerce others to be like you. Be true to yourself, your beliefs and goals. Power brands understand this already. Coca-Cola® will never try to become Pepsi®, nor would Apple® make venture to come across as another Microsoft® or Google®.

This act of being true, is nearly always humbling and life-changing. Because of this, it is usually the last strategic contrivance branding execs will undertake. It can be extremely difficult to identify and legitimize your core values to others.

And, allowing others to see the real you can be humiliating. Humility can be a powerful tool.

I was hospitalized for an on-going chronic health condition at a very early age. Even today, there are people who do not know how to begin a conversation with someone in a wheelchair. Silly things can come out of their moths. I realized, around the age of 8 or so, that I could release some of the tension, to make people laugh by making fun of myself a little. Hearing this laughter from other people became my form of rehabilitation, and theirs too.

Truth is powerful medicine, even if it is at your own expense. Comedians have used truthful self-deprivation for decades, using comedy to earn sympathy from listeners and enthusiastic rapport for their comical routines.

"I am so clever that sometimes I don't understand a single word of what I am saying." — Oscar Wilde

"I could never join a club that would allow a person like me to become a member." — Woody Allen

Never underestimate the power of the unostentatious truth. People that take themselves too seriously are difficult to be around. If, instead, you opt to use some form of flattery, brag about your devoted followers, never your own accomplishments. Don't worry, loyalists will see your intentions and get in line to congratulate, or compliment, you.

B. Be Inclusive

The slogan for the U.S. Army is, *"Be all you can be."* This sounds like a wonderful goal. Now I'm going to have to tell you why I agree. When the Army says, "Be all you can be", it certainly does not desire you to focus on the, "you", in this phrase, even though it states this very word in its mantra. After all, the only reason for you to perform at your best, would be so that you could better help others. And so, it might be better to say, "Strive to be your very best, so that others will benefit from your good qualities." This version is way too long, and boring, to be catchy motto.

The underlying meaning of becoming the best version of yourself, would be that this "better" self you are striving to become can better help others. Instead of realizing a (self-centered) dream, it might be better for you to help others realize whom they might become too. In doing so, you will be shocked how much you'll actually learn about yourself. Become inclusive, placing your effort on helping others will take you away from yourself, and highlight the ridiculously funny flaws that have kept you from advancing.

Expand your social circle. While not all people are likable, we do recognize that nearly everyone is liked by someone. So, begin there. If you are able to discover what that special something is, the "why", you'll have a great chance of understanding them better, and begin making loyal friendships.

I like to think of people as stained-glass windows. You will recognize their most important features when you can perceive the light coming from behind them.

Spend ten minutes a day differently. Walk your way through new departments. Go to a different Starbucks. Drive a different way to work. Then, talk about your new journeys with others. Help them to accomplish goals, small or large. Encouragement takes so little effort. Become a center point for imagination, where people around you feel inspired to succeed.

You'll be amazed. Great ideas come from the least likely places, and when that blockbuster idea does occur, you will be at its center.

C. Be Involved

Don't wait for others to take action. If you're an individual, join a club that desperately needs members. You will have skills that can be utilized. If you're a company, do something equivalent. Reflect on the possibilities of exploring outside of your familiar marketing arena. The most surprising and impactful changes will originate from without, not from within.

Inbreeding is a dangerous phenomenon that occurs in the animal world. It involves the mating of an unvaried group of similar creatures. This uniform direction will increase the chance for undesirable traits, and a decreased biological fitness in its offspring.

A social inbreeding will have the same negative offset in personal brands, as it does for wildlife.

If you are a technology company, see how you can support the environment, or a Little League team. If you're a company that supports senior health, invite young children or teens, and service canines to become a part of your overall elder care solution. I can guarantee you'll get support and more.

Remember this. You can't think outside of the box, unless you step outside of it first.

If you want to become popular you'll need to…
  A. Be Yourself
     Avoid the entrapment of celebrity status
  B. Be Inclusive
     Expand your inner circle beyond your range of sight
  C. Be Involved
     Take action, in a different or new direction

You've nearly completed this chapter. Congratulations on the desire to take steps in bettering yourself, or your brand. Popularity can be a beneficial and fulfilling goal to aspire, but is it your desire to survive, or to thrive? Is existing enough for you? I hope not. Because if your ultimate goal is to prosper…what you truly desire, is to better define your goals in life; your purpose in being; and to begin to learn how we - how our brand, our company, customers, and products fit into the world we live.

Les Brown is an American icon. He was pegged early on as simple-minded and illiterate — unteachable. Despite the self-esteem and confidence loss issues this created, he learned how to reach his potential with the support of his mother and assistance from a helpful teacher in high school. When it came to motivational speaking, Les was in a world of his own, knowing what to say at the right time.

This comment he made decades ago is so universally true. Positive thinking can have the effect of illuminating our possibilities, inspiring us to see past barriers in our way.

"In every day there are 1,440 minutes, that's 1,440 ways to make a positive impact. Too many of us are not living our dreams because we are living our fears." – Les Brown

As you learn to ask yourself why, to become more inclusive, and get involved, a productive metamorphosis will begin to occur. As you focus more on others, you will be inspired. Becoming self-aware, your confidence will grow. You will grow more adventurous, passionate, interesting and courageous. Surprisingly, you'll learn to laugh at yourself. Your popularity will grow, too. That monstrous social angst you once hid from others with a shiny smile will disappear, and people will magnetically be drawn towards you…and your brand.

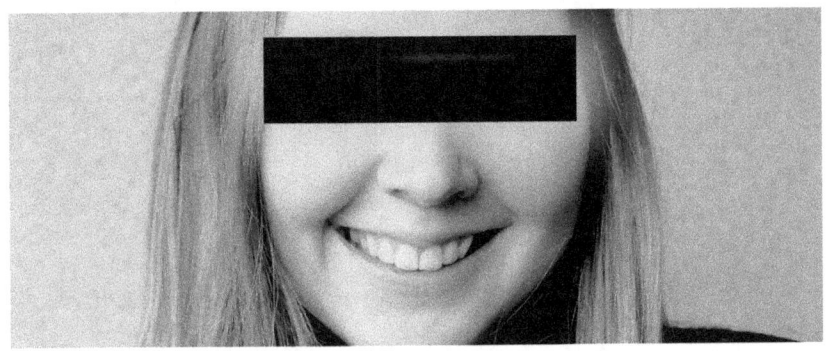

Chapter Two
Your Smile is Your Logo

People often ask me to explain what I mean by…Branding or Connecting. This is what I will nearly always say:

"Your smile is your logo. Your personality is your product. The feeling you leave others after having spent time with you, is your brand."

I like logos. I really do. I love creating them and looking at them too. I've take great pleasure in the process of crafting memorable ones. But, I've never, ever confused a logo with a brand. This type of mistake is often made, but is, mostly, an unintentional error by the unaware, or unknowledgeable. Those in the industry experienced in branding matters would never make this type of error.

Like a logo or a smile, a book cover can hint at what is inside, but it doesn't give commentary on the storyline. A mark, or company emblem, is just… a smile. A quick introduction. If you expect your logo to be more than a smile, it will do a huge disservice to the company, its employees, its products and goals.

I like smiles. I've seen some really great ones, but, I know that your smile is not you. Your smile introduces me to you in a visual way. It may create some fascination for me to connect with you, but it is not the connection itself. An interesting smile can keep me interested just long enough for a genuine connection to take place. I've seen inviting, interesting, devilish, and even quirky smiles, but I know a smile gives only a glimpse of what is inside a person. It's only the cover on the book, the shape of a car, or the screensaver on the digital display. Just like your logo, a smile provides only a clue, but still valuable information, inviting your customer to get to know you better. It is the first important step.

No, a logo is never a brand. It is an identifier of the brand.

Your Brand Should Be Smiling

Branding is a complex network of physical, emotional and transcendental strategies, but, at the heart of branding is a very simple component. People like to complicate things. I've heard many times the statement that the straightforward purpose of branding should be to 'partner' with consumers. If you believe this too, it's a big mistake. Customers should never be viewed as purchasers, adversaries, or even worse yet, trophies. The job of your brand is to remind them, that you already consider them to be smart, strong and respected friends of the company. Never view them as customers, clients… or even partners.

You may already agree with this statement. I don't want you to walk away with just an agreeable, yet casual nod. This assessment may be more important than you may first realize.

A product can only be considered a power *brand*, if customers perceive and associate something favorable when they think of your product. I'm sure this may seem like straightforward gospel to you, but while doing the work of branding, the simplicity of it is often forgotten. That is because the most important factor is also lost when it comes to connecting – customers are people, and like everyone else, have a deep desire to be treated and thought of as smart, strong, valuable and loyal. It's not enough to

LIKE your customers, or stay in touch with them…you must pursue them. You ought to consistently tell them how great they are, and how much you value them and their loyalty to you.

Everyone longs to feel good about themselves. To be valued. This constant pursuit we have to feeling esteemed and respected, is actually part of our innate human struggle to be recognized, and to be loved. We appreciate being pursued because it validates us. And, we enjoy pursuing only the things we truly love.

Remember this subtlety: People will crave to be recognized as intelligent, but they are not necessarily loyal to brands that make them feel smart. On the other hand, they will consistently follow imperfect brands that make them believe they actually have those character qualities – that they ARE clever, witty and astute. When you use positive, smart and strong elements in your promotion, your customers will perceive that you not only trust and value them, they'll believe you genuinely appreciate their friendship and their loyalty. Because you do.

Effective business branding is the art of building value right into your product, your service, and your people. Your strategy needs to be designed to communicate WITH, not TO, your people — your customers, your decision-makers, and your employees.

In order to succeed, your business revolution cries out for more than a logo. It demands a smiling face that is vision-centered, people-driven, and emotionally charged!

Chapter Three
You Are a Styrofoam Cup

Foam container cups have been around for a long time. Dow Chemical was the first to brand this Swedish closed-cell, extruded polystyrene foam in the early 1940s. Composed from 98% air, the material is lightweight, waterproof, and inexpensive to produce. Most people are only aware of the substance being used in drinking cups, bowls, plates, and food storage containers. Although this material is currently banned in some cities and counties in the United States, it is still used in a variety of other applications world-wide.

I'm a doodler. If you're anything like me, you like to play with your styrofoam cups, too. Especially after I've emptied its contents. It can be lots of fun because styrofoam is very easy stuff to leave nearly any type of impression on it that you'd like to make. You can draw on it, engrave on it, heat and bend or shape it into various forms quite easily.

One artist well known for his artistic illustrations is this guy known on the internet simply as "Boey" (iamboey.com). This previously unknown Malaysian illustrator, one day out of complete boredom, took a foam cup and drew all over it. I've done that too, as I expect you might have. After he began posting photos of his frustration cup art online, the demand soon came for more and more. Thousands of interests came in to purchase these from him. Now famous, he has trouble keeping up with the demand for his art.

That's cool, huh?

I don't sell my *frustration* cups, but still, I have fun marking them up in a variety of ways. I particularly love to make inscribed design markings on the lip and the sides of the cup. I do it uncontrollably. I've watched other people skillfully use the sides of their cup as a personal canvas with a pen or marker. Others will leave lip or teeth prints, cut shapes into the cup, or carefully stretch the cup sides into fascinating organic shapes.

We love leaving our mark, our imprint, on a variety of things.

In the early 1970s in a college public speaking class, I was asked to select a topic to speak about to the group. Rather than give just a routine speech, I chose instead to do something else. I chose an alternative method of *speech*, by documenting a social experiment. This was before social experimentation was common. I knew this might be a terrible gamble on my part, and my grade may suffer for it, but it was a wager that I was willing to explore, since:

    A) I really wanted a good grade in this class, and
    B) Why not? After all, I was living in the 70s, the age of freedom and experimentation

Prior to giving my speech I made a small request. Providing everyone in the room with an uninflated and individually colored balloon, I demanded that everyone in the class to do something, anything, with their balloon immediately. Once those in the room understood what I had asked them to do, the fun began. Nearly everyone began their task, by first giggling quietly, then laughing out loud. Soon after, many of them inflated their balloon with air, then taking a moment to observe each other, they decided what to do with it next. Out of eighteen students, three let theirs fly in anarchy around the room, one person did nothing at all, but fourteen students popped their balloon in a wide variety of ways, followed again by uproarious laughter. Some sat on theirs. Some popped it with a sharp object. Yet, others stomped on theirs.

You may have guessed, my class lecture was on *"The destructiveness of mankind and the choices people make prior to personal decisions."*

Everyone got a good laugh out of it. I received a decent grade for creativity. College was a fun place to get to learn your limits and be expressive too.

As I've already said, I can't help myself when I have a throw-away cup in my hand. I see it, and feel this nearly uncontrollable desire to do something, anything with it.

After all, it's a blank canvas that someone should fill. Most of the time I just tweak the edges just a little, but in nearly every case, it becomes difficult to abstain from transforming it in some small manner. One way or another I need to leave my mark on it. I draw images on it, scribe a design on it, crush it, or sometimes I attempt to make it pop by turning it upside down and slamming it down hard on a table.

Imagination is Infectious

Whether you believe so or not, everyone leaves a tiny impression in this world just by the fact that you are living. You are unique, and so the imprint you leave behind is one-of-a-kind also. Don't allow others to tell you differently.

Steve Jobs wrote, *"We're here to put a dent in the universe. Otherwise why else even be here?"* He's right. All of us desire this. Why else are we here? We love leaving marks on things. We get tattoos. We leave tire tracks in the dirt. We color our hair. We get that new car, suit, bicycle, or job that can change how people view us. In our eyes, singularity and uniqueness adds significance to us. We desire others to recognize us and the value we bring to the family, the workgroup, or the planet. It's our way of sharing things that make us unique. By making an alteration, though small or large, it provides the means for our personal brand and importance in the world, to bloom and blossom.

We Are Different, and Yet So Alike

People are a lot more like beverage cups than you might think. We are all styrofoam. We're not born hard and impenetrable. As much as some of us desire others to see us, in truth, we're malleable and squishy. We change as it suits us, or as time, others, or necessity alters us. It's not a bad thing that we mutate — it can actually be fun. Just like designing new tweaks on an extruded polystyrene foam temporary drinking device.

You are indeed a styrofoam cup. All of us are. But, is your cup unaltered? If so, should you modify it or leave it alone? Whatever you decide, remember that any modification will leave a semi-permanent mark that will affect every previous imprints.

In the same ways we choose to change ourselves, we're tampering with our persona, and increasing or decreasing its prospective value. By adding a bit of individuality to ourselves, we are making ourselves unique, brilliant, and worthwhile, or of less value because of personal choices.

When we make modifications to our personal cup — our personality, our skills, our integrity, our self-discipline and ambition become either priceless, or they can come to be useless.

That small dent in the universe that you'd love to make, becomes incredibly easy, or will be more laborious to achieve than you had thought possible.

How do you see yourself? How do others see you, your product or brand? Time to grab your cup and get busy.

Chapter Four

Pushing and Pulling

There is an important lesson we need to learn in the differences between pushing and pulling an object. To the unobservant, there may seem to be no difference in pulling or pushing, in that both are simply moving an object from one position to the other, but, the final outcomes are quite different and may surprise you.

I'm going to be sharing how I view this issue. As I've recounted in other chapters, the task of defining, forming and then keeping brand promises requires a multitude of coordinated minds, hearts, and hands. Leading a strong branding effort takes a deliberate contribution by all involved, not just the executive team, marcom staff, and agency creatives. Engineering, distribution, sales, financial and human resources... all people and departments will make a powerful impact on your ability to promise and deliver.

Even with a powerfully clear vision, your brand's love train can go off the rails. I have said prior that a vision was neither a path, a concept nor a solution. These time locked tactics may support your goals, but are not a vision. A customer-focused vision must include the values and emotional esteem by which your core customers define themselves.

While your vision ought to be true to self, it also must be immersed in a heavy dose of how your customers see themselves. You, at least, should show your ability to listen. Where we run off the tracks, is on 'how' and the 'why' we approach each task. The manner in which we probe, pay attention, present, and praise will make a big difference. How do we control these objectives? How can we calibrate our vision with our objectives. Here is where it might be vital to understand first, if you are pushing or pulling, if you are looking to build a bridge between this *how* and the *why*.

Pushing vs. Pulling

Steve Jobs was historically passionate about accomplishing great things, and so there were people who misunderstood his peculiar business style. Provoked by industry stories, many assumed his prosperity and success was because he forced people beyond their abilities in order to accomplish his goals. Although this type of interchange by pundits about him was legendary, I believe that this was never his underpinning intention at all.

"Apple is not about making boxes for people to get their jobs done," he said, *"Apple is about something more. Its core value is that we believe that people with passion can change the world for the better."*

— Steve Jobs

His goal was to bring out the very best in people — more than they themselves knew they could accomplish. His only objective was to make the very best products, with the very best people he could find.

I believe it took time for him to realize, but over the years he also learned the importance of depending upon the trust and help of others in order to accomplish these goals. Over the years, he learned an pivotal principle that Pushing did not work half as well as Pulling.
When pushing, you must position yourself from behind. Pushing a project places you behind the immediate view of the action, out of danger, but also out of the apparent

area of effort. When using this method, when you push the people who are working, they must be constantly looking backwards towards you, for guidance, but feeling as though they are doing all the work and you are tagging along for the ride.

Pushing is uninspiring because it requires a great deal of secondary effort, but no direct personal impact. At endgame, pushing is counter-productive because it causes those doing the actual work, to look in the wrong direction — looking backwards, and away from the critical task. In nearly every scenario, animosity eventually builds between camps, and productivity declines.

If you've spent more than a little time working or studying such trends in industry, you've experienced this chain of events first hand.

On the other hand, when you pull an object, you are required to be in the front and leading the way. People find following easier because when you lead, their path is laid out for them and they continue to look forward.

In business, pulling is easier because people are focused on following, not so much on the work they are required to expend. By leading you are not only showing the way, you are increasing productivity and loyalty. Great leaders pilot the way by leading – pulling, and bearing the psychological weight of the task.

I believe that this is why many revolutionary entrepreneurs appear so oddly compulsive. It is why they appear constantly busy, keeping their hands in nearly every facet of the business — to extreme detail.

There are many stories about the extent of Steve Jobs' complete immersion in a task; how he counted the tiles on a new retail store floor, or when he looked for design tangents on small products. The Apple Retail Store was one of his greatest successes. It was the first store of its kind to have usable products on display, friendly Genius Bar tech support help, and trainer-led learning workshops.

It is a unique people-centered approach to retail. Everything was important to him because all these things had an impact on people — his customers. He knew that the more he led the way, the more he learned about his business, his people, his market and himself, he could lead by pulling. Not by pushing others, but by pushing himself and leading the way, pulling his team behind him, and inspiring them to greater and greater goals.

Motivation vs. Inspiration

Motivation *and* inspiration is analogous to pushing *and* pulling. Like pushing and pulling, they may seem like the same description but the results are far different. Motivation and inspiration both stimulate in order to accomplish a mission or generate the same conclusion.

Motivating someone may be difficult, but inspiring them can be even more demanding.

You've probably heard the quote by Thomas Edison that, *"Success is ten percent inspiration and ninety percent perspiration"*. Imagining things is easy, but actually doing them is much harder. Take some time to understand the difference. Just as with pushing and pulling, whether you motivate or inspire will make a big difference on the end results you desire.

The danger in motivation is that it is usually counter productive. When you're motivated you feel strongly *compelled* to do something, because you're supposed to. The risk being that, motivation can lead in the direction of something that doesn't really matter to a person, because it only seems like a good idea at the time. Absence of passion, motivation is powered by an outside pressure, an obligation and/or guilt. Motivation may spike short term success, but, at its core, it is a false growth.

This is no way to build loyalty or sustain a valued brand.

Motivation is prodded by an external force, inwards on a mind, while inspiration is powered by an internal force, self-propelled outwards.

Motivation = Pushing
- Effort feels forced
- Duty, fear, and guilt override
- You feel obligated to act
- You are time centered
- You must psych yourself to succeed

Example: *When I try to motivate myself, nine times out of ten I'm pushing myself to do something I really don't care anything about.*

Inspiration, on the other hand, calls you to action because you are compelled to act. You seem to have no choice. Something inside of you burns with creativity, ingenuity, faith, and power.

In super alignment with your goals, you are energized and fulfilled *by* your actions, not just obligated by or satisfied *with* them.

Inspiration = Pulling

- Action feels effortless
- Passion burns steady
- You feel called to action
- You are team centered
- You are project aligned

Example: *When I am inspired, I see my potential regardless of what others think. This feels like a spiritual journey more than a hike. I feel refreshed daily.*

As we've learned, Motivation adds some form of constraint to meet a goal or directive. Now, that is not entirely a bad thing, if used measuredly. But, if you are hell bent on becoming a revolutionary leader, you won't see any benefit to driving cattle, or adding pressure to people. As Isaac Newton's third law states, force, even if used for a benign purpose, will have an equal and opposite reaction. Pushing will net a payoff that is contrary to your far-reaching purpose.

What is worse yet, when you are inclined to Motivate – your company, product or service, the team you work with, and you… have become time-centered, and secondary to the objective of your vision.

Inspiration follows your vision and energizes it along the way. It begins and ends with people. It is human inspired, human-centered, human scrutinized, and human electrified. It creates an enthusiastic esprit de corp from a potter's field.

So, it is clear to me that, in order to be a revolutionary leader, you'll first need to learn how to inspire.

"Everything around you that you call life was made up by people that were no smarter than you. And you can change it, you can influence it... Once you learn that, you'll never be the same again."

– Steve Jobs

Finally… when you lead, your co-workers and your customers must believe that you are inspired, and that you have their very best interest at heart. Once you find a way to merge your passion with compassion, you'll find it so much easier to inspire others, who will become captivated by your compassionate hardcore zeal, and joyously will follow your lead.

And, once they become inspired also, you'll be able to tug them to victory effortlessly by your example, and their loyalty will follow you to success.

Chapter Five

Inspiration and Realignment

I made mention of my urge to scribe on paper cups, or plates, in chapter three. I like filling pages too. I do also love how simplicity can be extremely beautiful, but my first inclination is to just fill a page, with words, ink, paint, scratch marks, or immediate thoughts.

Are you a doodler? Have you ever looked at a blank piece of paper, and somehow it just appears strangely empty to you? I don't mean in a minimalist way, I mean frigidly empty…plain and naked. Some people I know actually enjoy seeing empty walls, but I'm not one of them. For me, there nothing more pathetically agonizing than seeing the negative space on a living room wall, a white cup, or on an empty canvas. Like post-midnight 1950s television, it seems depressing to stare glassy-eyed into emptiness, whether it is a blank sheet of paper,

an unresponsive television screen,

a discombobulated computer display, or a fractured smartphone screen. Many people can relate to this last one. It can both bore and frustrate us to see all that nothing, in one spot. So much so, that usually, some of us crave to find any way to fill it with something relevant to us, or, if we run out of patience or creativity, we will just avoid looking at the object altogether to avoid the frustration.

This can make many of us just go crazy!

Unlike most of us, artists are semi-famous for staring at blank walls or canvases, waiting patiently for an inspiration to spark them. The post-impressionist artist Paul Cezanne was quoted to say, *"It is so fine, and yet so awfully terrible, to stand in front of a blank canvas."* Would-be artists, and students of the arts, have experienced this frustrating and anxious feeling also. Great artists are a very patient people. They need to be.

This same Paul Cezanne is known as a brilliant and greatly admired artist who changed the course of history. A few decades later, the great Pablo Picasso once commented that as the *father* of all modern art, Cezanne was the artist that showed him how to get in touch with his own individuality, and re-imagine the world he lived in. He credited Cezanne for his genius. I can be confident in saying that if it weren't for Cezanne, there would most likely have been no Picasso. And so, unknowingly, Paul Cezanne changed the world.

Perhaps this may surprise you, but, Cezanne was not always an admired artist. His amazing works of artistic expression were rejected on multiple occasions by the official Salon in Paris, and he was openly ridiculed by the art critics of his day, whenever, and wherever he exhibited.

Amazingly though, none of this mockery by his piers ever stopped him from filling thousands of empty canvases. He woke up every day determined to create, and by doing so he ended changing many lives forever.

Cezanne, and those with his type of spirit, never need to be nudged in order to search for inspiration in their work. Something hidden deep inside of them, kindles this unappeasable desire to smother an empty frame with personal feelings.

Inspiration is More Than an Inspired Quote

Most people are not like Paul Cezanne. I know I'm not. And, if you are anything like me, very few things could rouse you to his level of focused and animated passion. I feel the need to be inspired, or at least motivated, just to get my morning going. Just to make it to coffee. So, probably just like some of you, I begin, or end, my day by reading inspirational quotes. I also take some extra time to read books or articles, hoping to better myself in some way, and to create a *spark*. Occasionally I, myself, even write, hoping to inspire others. But, to be truly honest, I think I'm actually closer to everyday normal, the type that goes out and excitedly purchases pens, paint, a canvas and the matching easel…then only to be afraid to begin painting.

I want to be inspired, but I am fully aware that I'm not a laser-pointed genius, so…like many people, I have the most trouble at the starting point. How do I begin. I also know that if I am a little like that, I'm probably not alone — there are more people like me. If you're beginning to think that you can identify with me on this, don't feel guilty, or the slightest bit unworthy. Few people are born automatically knowing this stuff. We're not all Leonardo da Vinci, Warren Buffett, or Steve Jobs. It's OK.

From my experience as an educator and brand evangelist, I can offer you this. We first go wrong when we feel guilty for not becoming one of those prodigies we observe. *Questions arise*: Why were we not born intelligent, strong, or insanely imaginative? Why are we short, too tall or thin, or handicapped, or a color we don't like? Why have we been denied that one promotion that we've worked so long and hard to attain? Why?

We are brutal to ourselves and it shows.

I believe that this anxiety that we create in ourselves may be the reason why we have trouble succeeding. Why we have so much trouble waking up in the morning on weekends, and why we require that second or third cup of coffee on workdays. It can also explain why we are so easily distracted by such silly, unproductive, or nonsensical things.

We're average. It seems very obvious to us that we're very different from gifted intellects. Genius' wake up early and stay up late without prodding. Unlike us, gifted people come with their inspiration built-in. We don't. People like Stephen Hawking, Prince, and Bill Gates never needed to be nudged. We do. They were inspired. We seek motivation. Herein may be part of the problem, and the possible solution we desire, that and require.

You Have Such Great Promise

Some of you might be thinking that I'm wrong — that you are like that too…inspired. You're one of those special people who wake up early, stimulated and ready to go each day. You may indeed be, but keep this in mind… just being a quick starter does not make you an inspired person. While it can be true that once a brilliant person begins progress, they quickly learn to adapt and overtake barriers. But, the difficult issue isn't about starting, maintaining growth, or even achieving. You can be full of confidence, having all the energy, tools, skills and abilities, but, without knowing what fuels your beginning, you aren't living an inspired life at all. You may be gifted, but you're no genius. You've just learned to coexist with chaos in a spectacular way.

Whether your current hurdle is organizing a soccer league, solving a nagging software glitch, or taking an important lead in an emergency surgical procedure, the real trick to anything is knowing the *why* in your *how* to start. The *life manual* always leaves this out. When I say *how* I don't mean which way are you driving but, what drives you. When you think about it like this, the issue really isn't IF you're inspired, it's knowing what propels you to perspire…to go out and do the things you do.

As I said, focusing your energy is not the issue. Nor is it that third cup of coffee. Quite often we fail because we literally try too hard, place too much effort in traveling the wrong route, or get bumped off the path by forgetting what originally inspired us — the essential and pivotal, vision.

Beginning is difficult because those of us born with zeal, usually sprint head-long down the path without first being galvanized by a passion. Recognizing your vision, is vital to begin an inspired journey. Vision is more than the beginning and the ending, it includes the infuriating middle too. When your journey becomes longer, and feels more repetitive than you anticipated, you'll need the fuel that vision inspires.

As I've tried to explain, geniuses like Cezanne are inspired, while the rest of us desire motivation. To put it simply, They ARE, but we DESIRE.

Inspiration is very different from Motivation. Although both terms do sound the same, and most confuse these expressions for each other, without question, they are contrasting themes. While it is true that both motivation and inspiration stimulate in order to accomplish a mission or to move you to a conclusion, they, in fact, work contrary to each other. One generates energy, the other exhausts it.

Motivation Will Kill Good Ideas

The unrecognizable danger in motivation is that it is counter productive. Motivation pushes you in a different direction than inspiration. When you're motivated, you feel strongly compelled to do something, because you believe that you are supposed to.

Motivation is an exterior force that thrusts inward. It pokes and prods. Guilt, duty, and coercion are examples of outward forces that push inward to force a change. The nightmarish risk being that, motivation can take you in the direction of something that doesn't really matter to you, the family, or the job, because it seems like a good idea at the time. If you rely on motivation, you may find yourself on a path never knowing if, or when, you've arrived at your final destination. In absence of passion, motivation is powered by pressures from the outside, obligation and/or shame. It is in fact the enemy of peace, harmony and success. Motivation may have a purpose, but if you want to live an inspired life, please avoid it at all costs. Just to make myself absolutely clear on this one last time... *Motivation is fake inspiration.*

Inspiration Gives Life to ideas

Conversely, inspiration is powered by an internal force (within) that unconsciously, instinctively, and forcefully launches outwards. Inspiration calls you to action because you are compelled to act. Money, pride, guilt or coercion cannot persuade you if you are inspired. In super-alignment with your goals, you are fiercely energized and fulfilled by your actions, not just obligated by, or satisfied with them. You're keenly aware of what you're doing, and your day is animated from early morning, to late evening.

When you begin to prefer passion to obligation, you'll see people not customers, colors not data, entertainment not duty, and solutions not problems.

You'll Need to Be Inspired

Since you weren't born inspired like Picasso or Marie Curie, you'll need to find a way to place yourself on an inspired path. As I mentioned, I enjoy reading inspiring quotes, articles, and I sometimes even write them, but more than just simply fuel me, I use them to realign my purpose, my intent. My goal being to stay inspired and animated, not trying to motivate, or reanimate, any of my dead intentions.

Getting and living inspired means you are in a constant process of realignment. Don't allow yourself to be frustrated by this. Artists do this instinctually. Every mistake is a solution to another problem. Witty artist and television personality Bob Ross called them, *happy accidents*. *"All you need is the desire to make beautiful things happen,"* he would say.

Revolutionary entrepreneurs would agree. The heart pacemaker, penicillin, fireworks, and even chocolate chip cookies — all were mistakes that changed the world. If you want to live an inspired life you'll need to get your head straight. This (Freudian) instinctual id positioning requires less pumping you up, and more like feeding your inner desire for fuel.

- Whenever you're feeling like you have to push, it is time to realign.

- Whenever you're feeling like you're not enjoying life, it is time to realign.
- When you feel like you're trying to fulfill a quota or an expectation…it's definitely time to realign.

Here below are some powerful sensory benchmarks. These emotionally packed thoughts may help you to ignite your own inspiration, and avoid the constantly moving quicksand that motivation instills. Use them to help you to become realigned with your goals. Be…

Inviting - Expect something good to happen
Magical - Avoid solutions, and opt for awesome
Admirable - It must be sustainable and honorable
Gutsy - Look for the simplest truth
Identifiable - Be eagerly responsive, never reactive
Nurturing - Talk to people, not at them
Energetic - Always remain loyal to dreams

How to Stay Inspired

Realignment isn't complicated, but it does demand that you examine your motives and explore what it is that you really want. You'll need to tolerate being patient, just like you waited for Christmas morning as a child. You knew that something good was going to come. Remember…I don't mean, what you *should* want, or what you think might be a good idea. Work (life) has to excite you. If it doesn't feel good, then you haven't arrived. What is it that drives you forward, seemingly without effort? Once you've got a good grasp on that, stay with it for a little while. Think about why you might be perfectly fine by patiently waiting for something special.

I like to explain it in this way… *"When passion outweighs compassion, you'll see a forest instead of trees".*

If you can understand what I'm trying to say in this phrase, it will not only excite you, it should inspire many of those around you too.

Once you find a way to embrace your vision, your center of inspiration will grow. You will be surprised when you're able to accomplish some pretty amazing things. A wonderful side effect of an inspired life is that it is impossible to be contained. I like the way Pablo Picasso expressed it. *"The meaning of life is to find your gift. The purpose of life is to give it away,"*, he said. Did you hear that? He said it must be given away.

Mother Teresa put it this way, *"The miracle is not that we do this work, but that we are happy to do it."* You have all the tools to win the battle in marketing your products, or achieving your desires. Don't give up. Your customers are on your side, and they want you to be victorious. Begin your vision by connecting to them. Be inviting, magical, admirable, gutsy, identifying, nurturing , and energetic. Focus on those things that make you worthy of their loyalty. The steps you'll be required to take are embedded inside your vision, your people, and the desires of your customers.

While motivation can make you feel more introspective and pressured to meet goals, inspiration can cultivate inside, making you into a human-centered, people-powered revelation to others — an enthusiastic, esprit de corps powerhouse, worthy of loyalty.

Chapter Six

Pace Maker or Pace Setter

Perhaps you have never before been asked this question: Would you consider yourself either a pace maker, or a pace setter? Both descriptions seem to be positive in nature. Both generally describe you as a type of leader. But, when you begin to break each of them down individually, one of these titles may preferably appeal to you more. One may even rank higher in your judgment to the other.

Let's take a look.

If people were forced to make a choice, I believe most would rather be thought of as being a Pace Setter. They'd rather be known as someone setting the pace, than making or keeping a pace. A Pace Setter is out front piloting the way like a captain, or at least an intuitive and trusted navigator. Most of us may not always feel like we are one, but we'd certainly like to think that we can be, if we desired.

On the other hand, there may be excellent reasons why you should not overlook the role of a Pace Maker.

Olympic long-distance runners find it more to their advantage, in the long run, by keeping pace, staying safely and closely behind the pacesetter, waiting for the right time to take and hold the lead. A Pace Maker is steady and consistent, They don't waste their strength. Like no other, they understand how to utilize time and energy to their advantage.

In your mind, one of these types may resonate negative to you, while the other so monumentally superlative. Transversely, you may not think that either are an accurate description of your work personality. And so, to think you should be classified, cast in stone, into either one of these two, may be a difficult premise to settle into.

The interesting thing is… most of us could never imagine that we would fit into either classification. We can't see ourselves in this way. Or, you might imagine yourself neutral, the perfect blend of both, uncomfortable to be so defined. We hate this feeling of being pigeonholed, or cataloged, for this gives an impression that our fortitude, our freedom to choose, has been neutralized by our hereditary nature. We'd like it to appear to others that we are always in control of our decisions, and yet, remain impartially judgmental.

Both have advantages and drawbacks, it's true. But, can you be both? Are there times when it might require you to be both Pace Maker and Pace Setter?

Although this is generally the time when I will strongly reject bi-sectioning in favor of blurring the lines, in this case, I think I'm going to have to take a decisive stand by stating, what I believe, what is obvious to me. And, that is…

Revolutionary leaders find it nearly impossible to be both.

Successful, and powerful leaders lean heavily on their strengths. When you accept a leadership role, you will identify effectively as one type, or the other. The passionate personality of a true leader won't allow you to straddle the fence. If you're a blend of both, you are probably not a strong innovator or principal figure. I'm not trying to sound dogmatic, I know I will have dissenters who will object to this line in my thinking. I just really feel impressed about this, and hope I will be able to explain my reasonings to you in the following commentary.

How to Recognize if You're a Leader

I'm going to repeat my opinion. As ridiculous as this may sound, it is my belief, that generally, leaders will innately fall into one of these two categories – Pace Maker or Pace Setter. They will NOT be both. If you believe that this is to hard a line for you to maintain, and that lines between them can, and do blur, you might get me to agree, but only a bit. Most of us may indeed be a combination of the two, but then, I'm not speaking about most people. I'm talking about leaders, not followers who lead.

If being called a Pace Maker sounds to you, as though you may have some hidden character failures, compared to a Pace Setter, you'd be wrong.

Pace Makers are those who keep pace, who are always on time, are perfect on the details. They are immensely handy people to have around because, they know where everything is, and where it belongs. They are perfect file savers, clock watchers, and bean counters. They'll keep you honest. They are also rule keepers… No, they are rule guardians! If this description bothers you, and leaves you with an uncomfortable feeling in your stomach seeing yourself in this light, then it could be possible that you might be a Pace Setter instead.

Pacesetters are entirely different animals. They are pack leaders who are able to energize the uninspired, and turn monochrome into technicolor. Those who set the pace are those that lead the way and set a bright light on your path. But then, they are not without flaws either. They may appear as natural leaders, even corporate alpha dogs, but Pace Setters can often miss important details in favor of following a vision. Awe-inspiring as they are, they may be able to see into the future, but they can forget where they last laid their glasses or parked their car.

Like the terms inspiration and motivation, these two work labels can easily be mistaken for each other. Pace Setters can easily become confused with Pace Makers. The dispositions in both can become identifiable and/or exacerbated in times of stress or anxiety. Most individuals can hold things together, but these two individual categories of leaders have very low thresholds for doing things in the wrong way. Both have a disdain for dissension, and seek to be the first in line for nearly everything. In business, we talk a lot about *passion*. These two types are strong-willed individuals, way beyond what we might call *passionate* — they're *invested*.

But, there are definable differences that we can and should identify. Here is one divining rod. A single way to measure if you are one or the other... or you are neither.

If, when you are late for work, or you procrastinate on certain tasks, if you over-volunteer your valuable time, or you show up unprepared to meetings, and you feel just a little bit of shame or remorsefulness, you are neither a Pace Setter or a Pace Maker. If you feel even the least bit of guilt for your work habits, more than likely you embody neither approach.

Pace Setters and Pace Makers rarely feel guilt. Remember… I'm talking about revolutionary leaders, not just anyone. Pioneers tend to be pole-driven. The stronger the personality, the more success-oriented trailblazers will lean one direction or the other. The rest of us fall mid-ground, honorably and dependably picking up the daily pieces, for the torchbearers we faithfully follow.

Pace Makers

Pace Makers are leaders who invariably make the most noise. When I use the word *noise*, I don't mean they are annoyingly loud creatures, howler monkeys or long-tailed macaws. Nothing as literal as that. I'm suggesting that, as a rule, they seem to have an opinion, a critique, ready on every subject. They are businesses' task makers and are led by numbers. At the outset, they may appear to be uber-negative individuals. By nature, they are detail-driven people who see the nuances in every conversation; in the weather, the menu, the flaws in every product, in peoples' grammar, the number of nails used to build a house, or ones personal timing. Myopic by design, they will stare you, or your project, or the current highlighted issue, down with an open glare. They will get to the bottom of things. It may not always be a pleasure to work with them, but they are good to have around if you need a quick solution to a problem. These people make expeditious decisions.

Pace Makers are:
- detail oriented
- led by numbers
- people managers
- nagged by problems
- fast decision makers

Pace Setters

Pace Setters are very dissimilar in ways, from Pace Makers. Both may be goal-oriented, but as a rule, Pace Setters will typically see past you and your personal issues, always towards their ultimate objective. They can avoid examining the nagging details, if it suits them, as long as it brings them closer to *home* sooner. They see the big picture, even if you can't. They can be reputedly caught in a constant stare, seemingly inspecting the horizon instead of you, or their present footpath.

Their nature is genetically exemplified as being far-sighted, and they'll appear to ignore your existence, often coming across as aloof, seeing right through you. It's not your fault. They may actually perceive you being in the same room, but more often than not, you just happen to fall in the direction of their interstellar gaze. Just like Pace

Makers, they are excellent at coming up with solutions, but for far different reasons.

Pace Setters are:
- future focused
- guided by ideas
- vision managers
- agitated by details
- firm decision makers

I'm not asking you to select one to become, or to work. Both Pace Makers and Pace Setters can be revolutionary leaders… bright sparks who drive products, ideas or companies to remarkable heights.

This is not an either/or scenario, or a Catch-22. We may be able to survive without one or the other, but we cannot thrive. I've experienced both leader types in my years of industry involvement. My simple opinion is, that both styles have distinct strengths and weaknesses…and we need both to feel victorious at the end of the day, when we lay our heads to rest.

We need detail people. Those people that see between the cracks, the roots, or causes of a problem. People who wake up each day with there eyes keenly aware of what waits the day. Business scientists who love logic and the freedom that predictability brings. Our corporate warm, comfy, and cozy blanket. These people who save the rest of us from the drudgery of having to do the math, upon waking up each day.

We need idealists. Those who seem to live beyond our skyline, where orthodox mortals become disoriented. Visionaries who dream for the rest of us, bringing stimulated excitement to our uniform days. Leaders who can consistently persuade, even the weakest of us. Creators that will revolt against predictability, seeing art positioned in its proper place, as intensively written, invisible math. Those that by their true nature, have the deftness to elevate our eyes at just the right moment in time.

We need the rest of us, too. For those of you wondering where you might fit in, don't worry, you'll find your way organically. Most of us fall in the middle, part mathematician, penny-counter, master-blaster, manager and scientist. The other half of us dreamer, soul-searcher, astronomist, architect and artist. We may be relegated to being half-breeds, but we're important too. We're the ones that keep the car running, the daily maintenance, the roads clear, and the roadmap secure, so that the path can be enjoyable for everyone – even for the revolutionaries who lead the way.

I've often said that… *Rights and responsibilities are socially glued together, and once we separate them, someone or something suffers.* So, the question is never, either/or. There is no doubt that we need Pace Makers and Pace Setters. If we have plans to succeed, we'll definitely need both genres.

Pace Setters who will energize our cerebral cortex, and Pace Makers that activate our cerebrum. We'll need steely eyed task managers, compassionate bean-counters, evangelistic visionaries, artists and scientists, geologists and astronomers, all working in unity with the rest of us to observe, and to sort out, the unseen calamities that will wait for us tomorrow.

Chapter Seven
Failure is a Cruel Word

President Richard Milhaus Nixon wrote, *"Never let your head hang down. Don't pray when it rains if you don't pray when the sun shines."* It may be hard to believe that this president who was so nearly impeached by Congress, who was outwardly rejected by much of the country, and eventually run out of office, could come up with an uplifting statement like this.

When the going gets tough, it is so easy to give up. Most of us, at some point in our lives, have involuntarily listened to this sad siren song — melancholia. Millions of Americans suffer from this each year. Depression, confusion or emotional stagnation has, at some point, hit every one of us. Symptoms include irritability, loss of interest, restlessness, insomnia, weight gain or loss, and difficulty making decisions. As humans we go through some pretty stressful situations: stressful divorce, painful physical afflictions, long-term joblessness, inexpressible loneliness, and a tortuous self-worth. Once we suffer these kind of setbacks, it can seem easier sometimes just to stay down.

Humans are resilient creatures. We can take a huge amount of stress and yet, keep moving forward. How do we keep going? Some of us read inspiring novels or quotes, we listen to uplifting music, or remind ourselves of the kind words from a friend. These methods can help encourage us to stay on track. They can help for a little while, but nothing seems to stabilize our lives for long. It is easier to write or to speak words than it is to put them into action. I'm certainly not judging anyone or attempting to tell them how to live their existence. People's lives are so complex and their personal issues are too diverse to manufacture a single solution. One thing I do know however, is that being defeated is a daily, and yet a temporary condition. Giving up is what makes your failure permanent.

Stephen King / Author

Harry Potter author, J. K. Rowling, has been a recent success story. We've all heard the story of how she was a single mother on welfare, just three years prior to her humungous success. There were times when she didn't even have enough money to feed her baby. Talk about stress. Horror Icon Stephen King suffered as well. He and his wife, both being writers, worked multiple jobs, giving up luxuries like a telephone and a car, just so that they could continue their passion for writing. He and his wife had to borrow nicer clothes for the wedding, when they married. Before Stephen's ultimate huge success, he received more rejection letters for his works, than he could use to paper the walls in their entire apartment.

Jim Carrey / Actor

While only 14 years old, Jim's family was hit by some terribly rough times. It all began when his father had lost his job. Now homeless, he and his sisters, his mother and father, all moved into a small VW van, and had to park it on a relative's lawn. Can you imagine? Since his father had a hard time finding work, the young Carrey took an eight-hour-day factory job after high school, to help the family make ends meet. At age 15, he performed his comedy routine onstage for the first time in a suit his mom made him, and although he totally bombed, he was undeterred. He would park on Mulholland Drive every night and visualize his future prosperity.

It took a very long time for Jim Carrey to become an instant success.

Colonel Sanders / Restaurant Pioneer

Colonel Harland Sanders was fired from a variety of jobs before he even thought of the concept of becoming a cook. His story began at a roadside Shell® Service Station in 1930. During the Great Depression when no one had money for gasoline, he got an idea and decided to run with it. The gas station where he worked didn't have a restaurant, so he thought he'd serve chicken dinners in his tiny attached personal living quarters. Over the next decade, he perfected the "Secret Recipe" for his famous Kentucky Fried Chicken®, and moved on to bigger and better things.

Historically, we can look at plenty of examples to remind us not to lose faith in ourselves. Reading these stories can temporarily light a small flame, encouraging us to believe. In most cases, the warmth that tiny fire provides, can last a few hours, maybe a week, if you're fortunate possibly as long as a month. But, sooner or later, we'll lose our optimism. It's a vicious cycle we are in. Once a person consumes personal rejection for any prolonged length of time, failure and frustration can be all that they will expect. Worse yet, any small success achieved in the past, become a phantasm, a ghostlike moment of success mixed with a generous amount of failure. It can be disparaging.

If you have ever been afflicted by hopelessness. If you've ever felt unappreciated in your occupation, or stood by and watched the wheels of progress turn for everyone but you, if you believe that you fall into this category for any reason, remember you are not alone. I am not just writing this for you, I'm doing it for myself, too. We are in this together.

I don't expect that reading this chapter will help you much, either. As I said before, reading, listening, and talking won't get you out of your personal malaise. Even so, here is one thing that I do know is true… Giving up is easiest thing you will ever act on, and yet it is the worst thing you can ever do to yourself.

Inventor Thomas Edison wrote, *"Our greatest weakness lies in giving up. The most certain way to succeed is to try one more time."*

Persistence is Beautiful

Persistence does have a huge impact on ones success. Some of the most legendary triumphs in history came about by determined individuals, but, we don't see ourselves being anything like them. We're not packed with a super dose of self-control. We're not luminous geniuses, or feel like we are singly unique in the world. We're just average individuals trying to get through each day with dignity.

The good news is that there is a way for us average Joes and Janes to succeed just like the revolutionary pioneers we read about. We won't have to ask for a *Lifeline* call, or stress big time about a small decision. We won't have to be young and zestful, or old and wise. We just have to act.

"You're never too old to be young," Happy the dwarf would sing in the movie *Snow White and the Seven Dwarfs*. I love this Disney® quote! Turn of the century fiction writer Franz Kafka would've agreed. *"Youth is happy,"* he wrote, *"because it has the capacity to see beauty. Anyone who keeps the ability to see beauty never grows old."*

We may not see ourselves to be like them, but we are, *exactly like them*. Let me repeat myself. We are exactly like them! Excellence is not a measure of any good work. It is a habit you must practice daily. You can't allow yourself to look past today. Whether you are young or old, rich or poor, abled or handicapped, you have a today. Use it!

Throw away the regret that keeps you staring into the past at your failures. Guilt is a house without walls, a floor, chairs, or bed... absolutely no place for you to rest. If you feel trapped, and everyone has at some point, then change your direction. Remember this, although the possibility has been discussed for hundreds of years, no one has ever seen a perpetual motion machine. It doesn't exist. There will always be an end, and a new beginning.

I am average, just like you, but I can share this one statement to be true... I have never failed, because failure isn't falling down, it is staying down. Failure is only a word others use to make you feel bad. Don't give much thought to defeat. It may come regardless.

Beauty can be found anywhere. Taking action will do for you what nothing else will. If you can't do big things, then absolutely do small ones. Just act. To-Do lists are fine, but accomplishing simple somethings every day will set you up for success. It will get you out there in front of other people who will see the outstanding abilities you have, those that you probably cannot see in yourself. When (not if) they share with you, be ready to listen with your ears and eyes open. If you act… if you put yourself actively out there… this will happen to you.

Now, once you receive kind kudos from others, do share them. I don't mean tout the praises your receive from others. No, no…I mean do the same for others. Look for their abilities, not their disabilities. Try to avoid flattery and adulation, but share with them what is real.

Contributing in this very small way will benefit them, and you too. Your personal life, your career, and your outlook on life, will gain a degree of youthful momentum that you could never imagine that you were ever capable.

Chapter Eight

Why Some Brands Lack Maturity

Forgive me. I know that I may be giving away my main point to this entire chapter in the first three or four paragraphs, but please allow me this one personal gratuity, and then continue to read on to the end.

Viral marketing and Branding are NOT the same thing. They are not even close to being alike. Here's where you should begin to pay very close attention. When you get dressed in the morning, you begin with your underwear and socks, before you place on shirt or dress, pants and shoes. There is a process you've personally adopted that works for you. But, you are not your shirt or footwear.

They may help describe you, but they are not you. It takes more than just a quick visual to learn about your value system and passions you love. It takes a close-up and intimate connection.

Branding is like this. If you're in the business of promotion, or helping others to promote, never make the error of equating *getting noticed*, with *being seen*. In addition, if you are a company about to hire a new branding team, I urge you to look for a crew who, despite their age, pedigree, or exuberance, can stay above the shouting, hand-waving, and overindulgences. This is not elementary school, it's called branding, Connecting 101.

In general, we humans associate *attention-getting*, with immaturity. When a small toddler behaves outlandishly in a grocery store, or when teenagers erupt their typical moodiness and recklessness in a public place, these childish behaviors are clear to notice. We all know what mature and immature actions look like. Behaviors such as these never look cute or amusing for very long, and they rarely conclude with a respectful or dignified ending.

But, just as parents need to be aware, companies too should be mindful of immature branding methods by their staff, or agency assignees. The sophomoric immaturity of splash-marketing methods may get you some short-term attention, but it won't gain you, your product, or company, any respect.

Branding is serious business. It's not a party game for some frat-boy blowout, although at times it can appear so. Unless you're throwing a party for prodigies, no one should be web surfing for puppy videos or shock monkeys.

Some of the largest companies in the world have made the unfortunate mistake of seeking attention, rather than gaining respect.

HISTORICAL EXAMPLES

Coca Cola® went from it's inspiring, *"I'd like to teach the world to sing"* thunderclap advert in 1971, to it's 1985 opposite, with its *New Coke* ad, using spokesman and comedian Bill Cosby. Even though the new flavor they were pitching won all the taste tests, they lost customers by changing too much, too quickly, and too publicly.

Do you remember the creepy, Burger King® commercials around 2003? The one where the flat-faced smile in the *King*'s giant puppet-like head shockingly appeared at your work, school, and in your home bed. It was supposed to be edgy and amusing, but it really disturbed customers. This campaign gave the notion that Burger King® thought it was a rationale option to invade the privacy of its customers. People felt infringed upon, and potentially spied upon. They completely rejected the campaign, threatened by this approach. It was bad news for the company, until they created a new campaign in 2007, where it threatened to end the Whopper for good, reminding patrons what they truly loved about the company. Customers came to the rescue and returned. The ultimate message by Burger King was that they knew they made mistakes, and were willing fall their own sword, if required. Burger King listened carefully to its customers. Shortly after this campaign, the chain made a significant recovery in the war of the burger battle.

There have been many branding miscalculations such as these throughout history. You really cannot blame the companies who broadcast them. It's not entirely their fault. They trust the seasoned professionals who represent them, to protect their brand and communicate an accurate, powerful, and persuasive message to their customers.

This problem will arise when the all encompassing goal is to create an immediate attention, rather than it is to be heard. Even poor branding may somewhat improve your visibility, but visibility is not everything. Visibility is not about being noticed, it is about being seen and heard – at the molecular, spiritual, and the *emotional* level.

Understanding is much more difficult than observance. I liken being noticed — as getting attention, and being seen and heard — as gaining respect. In the same way, viewing the fireworks on Independence Day is perfectly understood by youngsters. It can be easier to get kids to watch, than it is to explain to them why we fire them off into the sky, on the same day, each year. There's a wide and blurry line between getting attention, and gaining respect. In branding, there's lots of discourse about visibility. I can assure you, for the most part, it will be time wasted. Visibility is not about being noticed, it's about being seen. And, when I say, *seen*, I mean you'll not only be recognized, you'll have certain expectations placed upon you, too.

If you are using immature branding stratagems such as these, you may certainly get noticed, but you won't be acknowledged in the ways you'd like.

Albert Einstein once said, *"I live in that solitude which is painful in youth, but delicious in the years of maturity."*

Be careful how you read this quote. Einstein wasn't talking about adolescence here, he was speaking of maturity and immaturity.

IMMATURITY

Self-centered

Can't follow directions

Can only think for self

Short-term memory

MATURITY

Considerate of others

Sees value in pathways

Can be an connected thinker

Long and short-term memories

Mature branding must leave a positive, not just joyful, impact behind. Problem-solving should always become integral to your brand character, as your company grows to maturity. I'm not knocking young brand creatives, but the lack of maturity that can occur at any age. I am aware of twenty year olds in their prime, and sixty year olds still in puberty. Branding isn't a catchphrase, a slogan hanging on a wall, or video blog screen. Branding is a style of connecting deeply to the consumer. It is alive. It communicates artfully, the heart and soul of a company, its products, people and customers.

The Art Exhibition Example

If you've ever had a great experience at an art gallery, you might better understand where I am going. You wander through the exhibitions, and you locate a piece of art that you find interesting. You give it a careful once-over, or twice-over. You may scrutinize it for a minute…or twenty if you are fascinated, but eventually you move on to notice the next marvel. You don't stare at it forever, or think of taking it home with you, unless you are Bill Gates or Warren Buffett. My point being, unless a particular piece of art moves you so, you may not remember it past the next three rooms. For this to occur, it has to connect with you on some deep level.

Remember this. Your brand is to business, what words are to humans. It is this first step in your interchange with your customers. You are in the business of branding and social dialog whether you believe it to be true or not. Analytics tell the story. More companies each year are desperately trying to add social exchange to their brand strategy mix. About half the companies in the U. S. say these social relationships have improved their marketing optimization, customer experience, and brand health… and yet, less than one fourth will identify their social optimization as mature.

So, what is maturity then? What might mature branding look like?

Maturity, is when you've reached the level to where you can say, "Thank you", or "I'm sorry", to those whom you've hurt, or have helped you in reaching the position where you currently occupy. Unlike an unsophisticated approach, which at its heart, uses deception — maturity is honesty.

Electing to use honesty takes a lot of courage, and maturity.

Turn of the century American poet Samuel Ullman, famous for his poem "Youth," was admired by both Japanese and American people. In one quote he gave special guidance to youths saying, *"The measure of your maturity is how spiritual you become during the midst of your frustrations."* This is good advice for company execs and branding groups alike. Branding should transcend what you see and feel, the emotional, and go on to inspire.

Never forget to align all your social business efforts with business objectives and priorities. Your brand must align with your vision, your products, and your customers in a spiritual way. Your brand must be positioned in a way to value each individual in a patient, cooperative, and compassionate manner.

Unlike a metaphoric reactionary teenage driver who is all gas and no brakes, remaining a mature brand professional will take thoughtful assessment, meticulous planning, and most of all, honest and respectful action.

Chapter Nine

What Star Trek Can Teach Us

Have you ever wondered why two (or more) normal and reasonable people, can find it difficult to get along with each other? Why does communication seem so problematic?

Half of the marriages in the United States and the rest of the world ends in divorce. What's even more hard to understand, is that, over three quarters of these divorced couples claim irreconcilable differences, as the reason for separation. Meaning...they can no longer come together long enough even to communicate with each other.

This chapter you are reading is not about marriage or divorce, but it could be. It's reasonable that people will have a diverse difference of opinion, on the very same topic. But, how can intelligent, well educated partners, or symbiotic groups, come to such dissimilar approaches, and do so without emotions flaring, when they have so much to gain by staying and working together towards a compatible goal.

Although they may appear to be in strong opposition, they're actually not. Their battle is not because they're adversaries, but because they process the same information, in far different ways.

Austrian economist, Ludwig von Mises, spent most of his life studying and writing on the incongruities of human choice and action. *"Men fight* (he said)… *because they are convinced that the extermination of adversaries is the only means of promoting their own well-being."* Many times, we will persuade ourselves to fight, rather than cooperate, because we view it as survival. This is due to the fact that, as living creatures, we are survival driven. Although we may be social creatures, our sovereign nature will override any apparent danger to self. And so…by character…we are following a pattern of repeating our divisible and detached inclinations.

Einstein said, *"The definition of insanity is doing the same thing over and over, and expecting different results."* His quote nicely frames this discussion.

Businesses can fall into the same deconstructive patterns. Building walls instead of tearing them down, or, demolishing things instead of reinforcing them. In golf, it would be moving the ball instead of playing it as-is. In a marriage it might be, avoiding a discussion altogether, rather than exploring it, despite their differences.

Data-driven personalities will usually avoid creative and imaginative approaches entirely. Some business people have the belief that efficient branding is always data-driven.

On the other hand, I've worked with plenty of think-tanks who will emotionally defend the creative brainstorm approach to strategic branding. I'd love to provide you with a singular partiality, but after three decades of experience, the dilemma I've arrived at is…both can work, and neither can work.

It breaks down to this: Statistics vs. Creativity (linear or non-linear)

These two differing human problem-solving approaches correspond with seemingly disconnected thought styles — the logical and the creative. Like Democrats and Republicans, or the Hatfield and the McCoy's, a superficial analysis will lead most to believe that these two thought methodologies are diametrically and eternally opposed to each other. Without question, we can see that they are, and yet, instinctually we know that symbiotically, they also need each other in order to survive.

Understanding Linear Thinking

The saying, *knowledge is power*, was first attributed to philosopher and statesman, Francis Bacon, yet, many persons have used variations of this quote to add extra weight to their brand of logic. Most of us admire those who are logical searchers of the truth. There is a reason.

Here is why:

> They seek the facts
>
> They scour the facts for truth
>
> They connect truths linearly
>
> They try to avoid ambiguities

We've all observed people like this. Star Trek enthusiasts have been captivated by Mr. Spock's ability to discern hyperbole from truth for decades. *Star Trek-The Next Generation* had its Mr. Spock too, he was called *Commander Data*. Both characters are in overseer positions, and are yoked instinctually to both truth and logic.

These futuristic left-brained characters are in direct contrast with those personalities in movies such as, *Blade Runner* or *Mad Max*, where logic does not seem to exist. We may admire logic, but we also seem to love viewing a good train wreck too. And, although we enjoy watching chaos in process, we nearly always prefer to imagine a future where reason is in control. Ignoring the truth, it appears that we cannot imagine a virtuous future without utilizing logic as a central guide.

Now, back to reality.

A turn-of-the-century french cubistic artist, Georges Braque said, *"Truth exists: only lies are invented."* This thought is enlightening to me. What he means is… truth exists — and, while it can be discovered, it is not created. This quote secures a linchpin for those principled linear thinkers. There's no doubt that linear or logic/data-driven thinking has its pluses — and that, information (or data) is primary, underscoring the point that for any logical process, that their must be a decided-upon truth, as an agreed upon starting point.

It is also comforting for some of us to use facts (or truth) to bind the beginning and ending of an open thought. If we were to begin the process with an assigned beginning and ending, then the ambiguous wide gap in the middle kinda seems to fill in itself. Once again, rationale appears to save us time and effort. The beauty of logic is that it appears to simplify our pathway from beginning to end.

I hope I haven't lost you. Here is where it begins to get interesting.

Like most things in life, it isn't always that simple. The beginning does not always line up with the ending. In this case, a type of checklist automation has become involuntary. An attractive part of a data-driven process, such as this, is that is appears to be time-saving. Because we value time as we do money (time is money), we tend to think that saving time is generally worth any potential drawback, thereby, using logic to solve a problem, saves us money too.

Since linear thought sees the world as black and white, the person using this style of thinking cannot easily create options. If plan A fails to work, then the formula begins to break down. Finding the middle ground or reaching a compromise is difficult because linear thinking is repetitious. Although statistical accuracy may be assured, since the planned outcome never changes, it can lead to increasingly diminishing results.

EXAMPLE

Those of us who consider ourselves thoughtful and logical, how many of us consider it an acceptable sacrifice, to purchase cheap unsafe tires, for our family auto? How many would secure their total life savings in a brown paper bag, or purchase an old bed mattress at a garage sale This is the same reasoning why we use food processors instead of chopping up food by hand, and why we drive automobiles instead of riding horses. Times change, and we are logical thinkers. We, incorrectly, value money as equal to time. And, quite often, time and money don't equate. If there's a problem existing with linear thinking, it is that, we can act as though there is only one solution, one path, and one destination.

I'm not belittling logic, or those who practice it. Data-driven people have a crucial function in any blueprint for success. Statistical models give us markers to show when we've gone on the wrong path, or have gone off-road completely. Once linear thought begins, and takes us down a certain path, there are a limited number of possible final destinations.

Creativity, on the other hand (or non-linear thinking) has no path. It may be frightening, but from time to time we need to leave the world of logic, and engage in non-linear thinking in order to solve a problem. In TV terms, as much as we admire Mr. Spock, it is essential that Captain Kirk is present, too.

Insights into Creativity

When we think of the creative mind we think of painters, artists, musicians — spirited independent thinkers who are comfortable living and exploring in lonely personal solitude. People with the creativity trait are often thought of as unstable free-thinkers. While it may be true that innovators tend to *see* the world very differently, it doesn't mean that all inspired individuals are like Bob Dylan, Vincent van Gogh, or Frank Lloyd Wright.

Some of us may be more like Warren Buffet, Mary Kay Ash, or Bill Gates.

This doesn't mean that the rest of us may be uninspired troglodytes, or monotonous androids either. While a great deal of us pride ourselves in being logical, all the evidence is actually in contradiction. We like to think of ourselves as reasonable and left-brained, while in reality we have merely learned to adapt and co-exist with chaos in a non-linear world. In a weird way we are more creative than we are logical. While there are no identifiable creative-type markers, there are some revealing quirks that reside in nearly all those of us with the creative gene.

- They daydream
- They love beauty
- They ask questions
- They take risks

I am sure you can see yourself in many of these categories. Non-linear thinking transcends groups or boundaries. When we look at the connections common between…say, artist Pablo Picasso and Apple's Steve Wozniak, they're not easily identifiable, but they exist all the same.

Although he was claimed to have made this statement, Steve Jobs didn't set out from the beginning to *"make a dent in the universe"*. He discovered over time that by thinking of customers needs first, the complex world of high-tech could be made uncomplicated, and people-centered. By working backwards, creating a way to simplify human-machine interactions, customers could enjoy a richer and more personal experience with technology.

Pablo Picasso's art transcended time and physical boundaries. His biomorphic sensual artwork added poetic social messages with regard to war, love, and political themes. Although considered very strange at first, over time he became known as a genius of modern contemporary thought, by transcending the limitations of realism. The benefit he made to society was that his art allowed others to see themselves removed from the known universe, looking at humanity from a distinctly atypical angle.

It may seem to you an unhinged concept, to search for unsafe, unorthodox approaches, but sometimes we, as a people, need this.

It can take a Picasso or a Jobs in order to create one of these new visions. It is, however, important to keep in mind that this *vision* we may crave, is not a specific path at all. It is a value system which will highlight the course you choose to follow. This vision gives us our reference point.

We Love Beginnings

Humanity loves beginnings even more than it does beautiful endings. Every path we take seems to have a starting point, a middle and a journey's end.

We prefer beginnings because we've lived with them our entire lives. We begin school in pre-school or kindergarten and move forward through the grades. We read the entire book, and we wait patiently to discover the ending. Our minds think, A, B, C, and 1, 2, 3 – in this order. As a society, we attribute real value to starting at the beginning, keeping to a linear, and well-worn straight lined path. We are trained at an early age to revere logic.

In direct opposition to linear thinking, creativity chooses to ignore any beginning, pathway or ending, and instead, works, lives and breathes in the ambiguous middle. Just like any book by Dr. Seuss, imagination has no path. Non-Linear thinkers recognize that a path may define the position and direction, but never the important destination. It does not have a checklist or end goal, except to explore.

As non-linear examples: the heart pacemaker, penicillin, and safety glass were scientific accidents. No one set out to invent Velcro® or Post-it® Notes.

Please, don't misunderstand me. Although I recognize there's value in a counter-culture, I'm not an evangelist for the hippy lifestyle. I'm just trying to explain why a truly creative mind can be more valuable than logic recognizes.

Rather than argue that one approach is more important than the other, I suggest that they are both integral to success, and on a bigger scale, life. Creativity can breathe life into a dead body, but Logic strives to discern life's meaning. Rather than limit reasoning to just one starting point, non-linear thinking allows us to consider that there may be multiple starting points, and numerous destinations.

Both approaches have benefits.

Linear thinking is logical

Logic's end-game is to examine

Linear thinking is compared to using the freeway

Logic means connecting the dots

Non-Linear thinking is creative

Creativity's end-game is to explore

Non-linear thinking is taking the backroads

Creativity means creating the dots

As you can observe, both lines of thought have benefits and drawbacks. As a company, it is just as important to have goal keepers, as well as game players. To keep fresh and stay innovative, organizations need to be both controlled, and shaken up repeatedly. You'll need champions in each business area who aren't afraid of setting goals, and yet, able to venture off the path when required.

Would you be comfortable in saying that, only a woman can truly understand another woman? Following this line of thought...candidly, is it possible for a single woman to understand all men? Linear thinking tells us that it is possible, but down deep we know the truth. *"Life is really simple,"* Confucius said, *"but we insist on making it complicated."* The truth is, people are complex. And, communication IS complicated. Any solution, fusion, or compromise takes both exploration, and cooperation.

Businesses tend to consider their logistical and financial teams, as their logical thinkers… and the marketing and engineering groups as their creatives. Let me be frank with you. If you follow this rational, you are placing dangerous limitations on your company, or brand. You'll need to challenge every team to be as creative as possible inside of the box, or find a way to crack open a new one, despite the dangers within.

You've figured out by now that, I love to speak on the subject of branding. Why? Because, branding is simply this…creating dots, then finding ways to connect them.

President Harry S. Truman said, *"It is amazing what you can accomplish if you do not care who gets the credit."*

Creativity creates interest areas… dots. Logic helps in connecting these dots linearly (we consider them linear because they lead to a goal), rather than randomly. The aim is to identify the connections that link creative thoughts, feelings, loyalties and then formulate them into linear (logical) quantifiable connections.

You wouldn't restrict use to only one side of your brain, would you? Branding is both, a left- and a right brained effort — logical and creative. Power branding recognizes the value of combining data with emotional triggers. This is the rosetta stone of branding to humanity.

Rarely do these two abilities reside in one singular, specially gifted person. More likely than not, they co-exist in parallel, gifted individuals or groups. It is vital that they work together, share openly, and respect each others gifts as they do their own. Just like the human brain, in order to accomplish extraordinary achievements, they must first learn to co-exist in chaos.

Here is where both game players and goal keepers work together to play a huge part in a successful outcome — and where a captain hell-bent on fearless exploration, feels somehow compelled to insure that he always has a logical first officer close nearby.

Chapter Ten

Feeling Is Not Believing

Campaigns throughout history have attempted to use one or more forms of reasoning in their branding and advertising campaigns. These efforts are driven by leveraging logic to engage customers to ignore both truths and their natural senses. These strategies many times utilize negative pressures like physical fear, or fear of loss to make a point. This tactical use of logic or fear to avoid a potential threat, is a powerful method that forces a call-to-action by a consumer.

Let me be clear to you how I feel about this. Although there are many proponents of using fear in advertising,

I am not one. I believe using methods that motivate human emotions, characterized by the absence self-control, do not build long-lasting brand strength.

EXAMPLES

The World Wildlife Fund® and ASPCA® both use disturbing and powerful images to cause an end-of-the-world rationale in order to clarify their points. An unwashed kitten or puppy will go a long way to stir your pangs of conscious. These *'guilt'* campaigns can yield large donations.

Using similar techniques, companies who market security, such as ADT®, McAfee®, and Brinks®, will use fear to drive home a sale, and get you to purchase their products.

Nearly all companies have at one time or another, have used the leverage of fear to push you to act.

Nearly all of us take notice when we see a sale sign. No one wants to miss out on a great deal. When they read, 'Ends Tomorrow!', or 'Today Only!' we are driven to look. Negative branding is widespread because to some degree, because it works. Since this does the job, companies and agency creatives ignore using positive intent and human emotions when it comes to branding their product or service. They do this because it's simply easier to go negative…or to go with using fear as motivation.

They forget that it is strong, smart, and loyal people that purchase their products, and not vacuous, guilt-ridden robots. Customers will always prefer to think they are strong, not weak…smart, not ignorant… and loyal, not automatons. They will reject being talked down to, or made to feel guilty. It can tick them off. They may end up purchasing your product for one reason or another, but they will not be loyal.

Fear is a Dangerous Emotion

You should be cognizant that fear is not a sense, it is an emotion. Emotions can be very dangerous because they, and their resulting outcome, can be difficult to predict.

Once we use emotion to sell, we have to be extremely careful – because we're walking on a thin tightrope. If we use emotions or feelings to brand a product or service, we have to be sure that ultimately, our motives are positive in nature, because the ultimate outcome will last a long time.

Physical Senses Are Neutral

Every customer has five fantastic preceptors from which to make decisions: sight, hearing, taste, smell and touch. The human senses are a perfect launchpad for smart branders, because they are sensory neutral and distinctly human.

Much like fear, logic does not make very good branding sense either. If it did, I'd be seeing strong inductive, adductive and deductive advertising campaigns by power brands all over the TV and internet... and I don't. Weak brands use fear and/or logic to sell, to add value, or to create urgency. But, in general, humans prefer to push fatalistic feelings away, and by doing this, they will prefer to forget ads that portray negative feelings.

Fun Can Be Fun

Then again, some companies decide to create levity in order to inspire sales. While this may be a step in the right direction (at least it is positive), it is not enough. You've likely seen advertisements that you enjoyed watching, and you remember them making you laugh. Data has shown us that although people do enjoy laughing at advertising, they would much prefer if you made them to feel smart.

We all have favorite commercials we've seen, but we forget the names of the products. If the goal of advertising is to be memorable, we've failed. We must remember the main goal of branding. It is to be memorable — with a guided purpose. The ultimate ambition for a brand is to be able to justify the reason for the company's existence.

I'm not saying that we can't have a little fun, or use humor in branding. This type of communication can be quite effective if used appropriately, and smartly. An example would be — to ensure viewers feel that they are 'in' on the joke. Your promotion should be an invitation directed towards smart people who grasp your benign intentions, and laugh right along with you.

Let's not let this proceed with just an agreeable, yet casual nod.

A product can only be considered a power *'brand'* if people perceive and associate something favorable when they think of that product. I'm pretty sure that this concept seems like straightforward gospel to you, but the simplicity in it is often forgotten. This is because the most important factor is also lost when it comes to branding – customers are people, and have a deep desire to be treated as smart, strong, valuable and loyal.

It's not enough to stay in touch with customers, you must pursue them — to consistently tell them how great they are.

Everyone likes to feel good about themselves. This constant pursuit we have to feeling better is actually a struggle to be recognized, and to be loved. We love being desired. We enjoy being pursued because it validates us. Remember this subtlety: People are not loyal to brands that make them *feel* smart, but they will consistently follow brands that make them *believe* they actually have those character qualities worthy of desiring.

When you use positive, smart and strong elements in your promotion, your customers will perceive that you trust, value and genuinely like them too. There is no better way to build and maintain loyalty.

Chapter Eleven

Social Branding and Privacy

Friends of mine know how much I love wristwatches. So, the other day, I went online in search of a new wrist piece. I searched and clicked, exploring a number of sites. I couldn't find what I was looking for — so I left a little frustrated, as I usually do. Almost instantly... hiding right there in plain sight, some crafty code noticed my unhealthy interest in watches. Nearly at once, it seemed, I was besieged by alternative purchasing *suggestions*.

If this story sounds a bit like your online life, you can see, you're not alone.

I am sure you've noticed how the internet seems to know what you are interested in. Everywhere you go in cyberspace you're besieged with offers. Every company hopes you won't refuse to click, and add their product to a shopping cart. It can make you feel stalked, like a proverbial celebrity, but in the worst possible way. Not because you're famous… but because they just want your money. They seem to follow you everywhere. You cannot shake them.

Miners and Schemers and Bots, Oh My

Every like and dislike, everything you search, follow, or ignore, is compiled by real or robotic data miners. This data is compiled from your public records, credit card transactions, grocery and clothing store savings cards, photos you take (whether you share them or not), social media interactions or internet searches. This information reveals where you shop, the food you like to eat, movies you go to, who your friends are, the places you go, and which brands you prefer. Also, linked within is demographic information like your age, whether you are married and have kids, your college degrees, which part of town you live in, how long it takes you to drive to the store, your estimated take home pay, whether you've moved recently or planning to relocate, which credit cards you carry in your wallet and, of course, the websites you commonly search and which select to make purchases.

You cannot seem to keep away from these nasty critter-bots. What about your right to privacy? It can be extremely annoying. Nearly every online retailer or major brick and mortar, from grocery chains, department stores, coffee houses, investment banks… even the U.S. Postal Service has a predictive analytics team devoted to understanding your shopping and personal habits.

This sounds like a movie plot that we've seen before. I know that many people are obsessed with watching melodramas, but this one seems downright creepy. Can it really be this bad? Is this a shocking cinema storyline gone awry? Just to think that some guy might be sitting around in a dark room waiting for us to do something so he can throw up an advertisement surgically aimed at us.

Another scenario would be that it's all about *Sky-net*, an artificial intelligence in our networks, learning as much about us as inhumanly possible, so that a coordinated robotic synergy can compile enough data from us to take over tomorrows humankind.

We've all read about the Russians and Chinese hackers, and their lust to destroy our freedoms. I'm not saying this is as far fetched as an old movie plot, nor is it trifling…it is important! We know it is happening, but maybe not as we have imagined. We assuredly need to arm our internet with the same fervor as we do our military. Every loyal American citizen, in government and in business, must be aware. What I do mean, is that for the most part, you specifically, are not the enemy or whom they are afraid. Foreign governments are more interested in Washington, than they are in Boise. Fake news may be able to rip a hole in the fabric of real news, but it will take more than this to destroy the foundations of American generations. And, this could only happen if we allow it to polarize us first. And, hopefully we won't.

As for the weird movie plots, let me reassure you: there is no T-800 from the future, planting present day advertising to allure you. Likewise, there are no darkly hooded lowlifes in low-lit bedrooms (dark or not), for the most part, personally watching every move you make online.

Allow me to pull back the curtains and reveal The Great Oz. You might be surprised at what we find.

OK, here is the magic.

Behind all the mysteriousness we worry about, it's all just code — ambiguous phantom-like flying sets of ones and zeros on the information super highway we call the internet. The same kind of code that allows you to search for stuff, is the same type of process that allows others to remember you. Well, not really YOU, but the things you find important enough to look for. When you look behind it all, it's more like a mirror, than it is a menacing monster in the closet.

Let me ask you a question. Do you like it when friends remember your birthday or favorite food? Of course you do. When you search on an internet-capable device, it too remembers what you like. It adds a *reminder* to your browser. They call it a *cookie* because who ever turned down a cookie? I don't think I ever have. Sure, cookies can be good or bad, but remember, you don't have to take one. When you think about it, the idea that people get creeped out by cookies seems kinda funny. You'll always remember a good cookie, but in this case, the cookies will remember you. Sounds nice, and it can be.

There are Good Cookies and Bad Cookies

There are some cookies that people should like. If you don't believe so, here's why you probably should.

People are creatures of habit. I know I am. They tend to repeat their lives, day by day, year by year. They routinely go for the same foods…wear the same type of clothing… buy the same toothpaste. Most often they vote the same political party…go to the same church…and raise each of their children in the same way. Families, cultures, and environments all play a huge role in delineating what makes your life ritualistically habitual.

Subconsciously, humans do this for two reasons:
    A) they tend to prefer uniformity to chaos, and
    B) a routine life simplifies living

We enable this process. Well, our brains do. Psychology has a name for it. It's called chunking. *"Chunking"* is a short-term memory mechanism the brain uses to help it to remember. An important thing to take into account is… we're like this because we really do like our habits. We're comfortable with who we are, what we like, and what, and who, we don't like.

This process, chunking, occurs when the brain transforms a sequence of actions into a regular, compacted routine. There are dozens, maybe thousands, of behavioral chunks we rely on every day. These patterns save us time. They simplify our lives. They can even protect us from danger. Some are as simple as placing toothpaste on your toothbrush before sticking it in your mouth, or buckling your seatbelt before starting the car.

Many of these actions happen without us being aware. Unconsciously, people are desensitized by their patterns of behavior, preventing their psyche from being aware of this process. Since our brain loves routine procedures, *chunking* enables automatic time-savers for us. These self-imposed loops, or life patterns, begin to take over our lifestyles. This apparent lack of awareness that this is happening, is what can creep us out, scare us. Being aware that this happens may upset us, but it really shouldn't. What we cannot see, is that WE are in the authority the entire time.

Who's the Boss?

An important fact to keep in mind is that data itself is not dangerous. It has no intelligence. Data is just a mix-mashed collection of information, facts and knowledge. It's not alive. Data only has meaning when it makes sense to you — personally and individually. Data (mining) collection can be a good thing for people who love their habits — their chunks. In fact it can become very beneficial, if utilized as a phenomenal time-saving tool. Let's take a look.

The action within our brains that creates these inclinations (chunking) is a three step process.

The Trigger

First, there is a trigger, a simple marker, a touchstone that tells your brain to go into automatic mode and which habit to apply. It can be a color, a shape, a sound, or a sensation. This trigger may begin from without, but it is created inward…entirely by you.

The Pattern

Next, there is a routine pattern, which can be physical, mental or emotional in nature. Triggers motivate you into following a framework of these preferred signposts. These are organized mental artifacts that your brain has already approved of in the past.

The Reward

Finally, there is the reward. All life, including humans, never do anything without a reward. The payoff in this case is one that helps your brain decide whether this particular pattern is worth remembering for future usage, or not. Most triggers and rewards, in fact, happen so quickly and are so slight that we are not even aware of them. But our neural systems notice and use them to build instinctive behaviors, and/or emotional patterns.

Over time, this *'loop'* — a trigger, a routine, then a reward, becomes automatic, self-activating, and instinctive. These triggers, patterns and rewards become organic. Once organically animate, it can quickly become, in a peculiar sense, unconscious. We might better refer to them as desired habits, because we are never bound by them. We are in complete control the entire time. Like loops and chunking, a *cookie* might just be one of the best friends you ever made.

Your best human friends will follow these same actions. They learn what you prefer, and then do their best to oblige your shared likings. If you change your mind about something, they'll learn and avoid sharing it with you.

Social branding does not create chunking, you do. It just takes advantage of it, adding benefit should a person choose to accept, and reward the pattern. Since our rituals are mined and tracked, branding only assists people to be better aware of their preferred patterns. Once in touch with what triggers us, we can replace them, if we like, and… just like a heavy wool coat in the heat of summer, the old markers will lose their purpose.

Social branding can serve the same function as a best friend. In this endeavor, social marketing and/or branding might just end up becoming one of your best friends too. In a non-judgmental way, social branding takes advantage of these ritualistic behaviors that we all have, and uses them to communicate better with us.

Communication is the Bedrock to Trust

Here is where smart brands can benefit and gain an advantage. Social marketing adds measurable value when it takes the high road. Astute businesses should make this a personal call to action — a test of loyalty. Their solitary purpose should be to help customers to save time, and make wise and timely purchasing decisions. As an advocate, permeated with transparency, every customer connection must be to benefit a loyal friend.

This should be the ultimate goal, to value this friendship, and to serve, not just to sell. When this type of loyalty is achieved, the once hated reminder *cookies* that customers perceive daily (ever observing, labeling, counting and measuring), will be seen for what they truly are... as just affectionate reminders.

For us in branding, this will be an important lesson for us to learn. If we ignore this example, shame on us.

If our goal is to reassure devotees, rather than quantify subscribers, these self-compiled thought chunks, these packets of customer data, must be permitted and enabled with the expressed purpose to benefit our committed customers, and not just become a database cauldron for our company, and our marcom's analytical staff.

If it is possible to become friends with our customers, saving them time, enabling them to make better decisions, then we can, and should, always respect their privacy too.

Empathetic power brands, have shown us that this is not only possible, it can be financially preferable. If we can create a positive way to save and share this data, with the purpose of helping to enlighten and empower our customers at each interaction, then every future connection we initiate with them will be observed as an amicable partnership, and we will be seen as less like a sentient cybernetic dark overlord, continually observing customers from behind invisible curtains.

Chapter Twelve

Your Artsy-Fartsy Creatives Deserve Better

There are supremely gifted people everywhere, in every corner of the earth. Some of them become physicists or mathematicians, artists or musicians, surgeons or business entrepreneurs, teachers or tribal leaders. Each of them come with talents that help them to overcome career obstacles in order to accomplish some very amazing things.

Over the past three decades, I have observed an interesting observation, with regard to gifted individuals. Except for the occasional lightning-strike historical occurrence, dissimilar prodigy intellects rarely will unite, or collaborate with each other personally.

It goes like this…

Artists tend to hang out with other artists or creative types, and entrepreneurs with others like themselves. In political circles we observe Democrats and Republicans repel like oil and water. Similar to high school cliques (remember them?), they gravitate towards like-circles of influence. Seldom do we find contrasting talents taking up the same physical space, even to share a table at a coffee shop. It is a rare thing to see dissimilar intellects sit together to pool their common resources, even if it is just to get to know each other better in an indirect way.

Why do you think this is? What keeps them from engaging with each other? Is it just because they are a different breed of intellect, or can it be something else entirely? Do they speak a separate offbeat language, are they just socially incompatible with each other, or is there another reason that this kind of disengage occurs?

They have more in common than they know.

They're not ignoring each other as it might appear. I cannot ever remember sensing any purposeful aggression. The disconnects haven't transpired willfully. Communication has not broken down, nor have I noticed scheduling issues preventing them from connecting with each other.

My guess is that, in a subliminally clouded way, they don't identify each other, because they can't even *see* one another.

Dialog between them hasn't even begun yet. Each faction remains in its tight circle, becoming invisible to the other and its core values. When neither side observes the other, its merit, nor feel the need to understand them or their slant on the subject at hand, a form of invisibility occurs. As far back in time as we can comprehend, there has never been a breakthrough in our ability to communicate intimately with a fourth or fifth dimension.

Those of us who observe this phenomenon taking place from the outside, who may be able to perceive these non-events occurring, will probably conclude that this is simply just the way it is. Others will just see people as being different, and that is okay with us. We'll chalk it up to us celebrating individuality. But, in reality, this lack of communication between academic sects materializes because those of us on the exterior don't see these conflicting cabals in the same way either. Like everyone else, we've segregated these factions into mismatched individually wrapped packages. It is because we allow ourselves to perceive them as separate and unique, with their own individual significance, that we, by our passive attitude, solidify the unobservable walls that divide them. These indiscernible and imaginary barriers that we unconsciously allow, isolate our brightest and best. Reinforced by the rest of us, our non-action prevents unity and growth. And, worse yet, it calcifies any and all attempts to bring contrasting disciplines together, to coalesce in a common goal.

My hope is, by the end of this chapter, you'll see how you might have been unconsciously incognizant of this, and look for ways to bring about a change within your own circle of influence. How a business entrepreneur might benefit by spending more time with a creative, a physician with a barista, or a senator with another member of congress. By doing so, by recognizing that there might be another box alongside yours, I am hoping this might make a positive impact in your own life, and those with whom you come into contact during your average day.

This great polarization circle issue might be starched and pressed into the Washington DC crowd, but it never originated there. It isn't a heritage born problem, or a societal one either. You should remove the personal choice excuse as a cause for the most part, too. The unfriendly agent, or corrupt source, has been hiding out in the open, right under our noses for nearly a hundred years. I believe education, our academic structure may be the problem.

As an ex-educator, and one who loves the process of learning, you might think I should be the last one to make this type of claim, but all the signs (in my head), point to this as a potential causation. It might also hold a possible resolution to this destructive social discord rerun.

I hope so. Allow me to explain. Read on and see if you agree with me.

To STEM or Not to STEM

America has fallen far behind the rest of the world for years in key education areas. In recent times there has been a big push to include technology into the classroom. We've decided to call this advocacy STEM, a curriculum based upon the idea of educating students in four specific disciplines; science, technologies, engineering, and math.

Pres. Barack Obama added his blessing to this plan during his time in office. The goal of STEM education is to help provide a new methodology, instructing our students to think deeply, so that they have the chance to become the innovators, educators, researchers, and potential leaders of Americas tomorrow. It is a good plan striving to educate our children using diverse disciplines, especially when they are young, and have wide and assorted interests. But, I'm going to throw what I think may be a small wrench into this accepted, adopted, and blessed new formula. Will you allow me to offer this motion? I promise you, I will try to make a constructive point.

STEMing or MESHing

Let's back up in time a few decades. Up until recently, general high school or college major coursework has been a combination of math, english, science, and history (social studies). Other than electives, nearly all core subjects were merged formulations based upon these four main topics.

Keep in mind…each of these curriculum plans come shrink-wrapped, and vacuum-sealed. Like vegetables and fruit on a plate, we prefer to keep them separated. Rarely do scholastic disciplines collaborate on projects or subjects. Math and english classes, art and science classes, history and grammar classes — remain sterile and separated, and for absolutely no apparent reason I can surmise.

Just as in a social caste system, there appear to be high-tier and low-tier studies. High-tier modules are considered core educational requirements, while those classified low-tier or electives, may not even be required. Math, english, science, and history were classified as MESH classes. Every other programs were deemed electives, optional. So, unless your major study area is in Art, you will likely never take drawing, painting, or a principles of art class.

On the other hand, even if your school major is Art, you will be required to take MESH or STEM courses, in order to graduate with any type of degree. Even if you happen to be focused on seeking a degree in Fine Art.

OUR HISTORY

Our divided educational framework begins early in our school life, and carries all the way through to our work life. No one ever intended this should happen. This pattern has evolved early on into a propensity that we've grown accustomed to, and have never seen a reason for it to change. Once we get an accounting job, we rarely talk to anyone outside of our job title. The same goes for engineering, marketing, operations…and creative.

This deeply rooted routine is one of the factors that disincentivizes collaboration between disciplines. It has become counterincentive for scientists to collaborate with artists, or mathematicians with politicians. The damaging consequences that ensue, result in a systematic professional detachment, and the social disparity we now experience. Continuing in this phenomenon will keep us separated. This separation, is the very thing that has created this polarization that we say that we hate, in the first place. If we truly disdain this cold social atmosphere we've created, you'd think we'd find the cause and eliminate it.

We should and we could, but the solution is equally painful. In order to eradicate social division, and solve the difficult social and economic issues ahead of us, it will be imperative that we first find a way to come together…long before we will ever find a way to work together.

First things first…I believe there is a way.

The Three R's

Although I have been part of the business world for three decades, and an educator for a few more, in general, I think of myself as a creative, an artist, who specializes in media and retail communications. For many of my early years, I wondered how my life might have been different, had I not studied Rembrandt, Renoir, and Rousseau (the three "R's" in artistic education). What if I had dived directly into business modules and teacher training, completely avoiding the physical arts of painting, drawing, sculpture, stained glass, ceramics, metal etching, and illustration? How might my professional life be different today? How might I be different personally, too?

When I look backward on my educational history, I observe that students of the arts seem oddly distinct from the rest of academics. They appear to be wound less tight, or more tight in other ways, than other fledgling scholars. But, for the most part artists are not considered serious students. They are not given the same type of approval gratis that students of science, math, and business students have traditionally enjoyed. I know. I was one. We were rebels, cloud heads, and over-sensitive artsy-fartsy types.

Math, science, history, and business students were most respected, while fine art students were gently tolerated. Artists in all ages, but especially those during the 1960s, were known as agitators focused upon disrupting the status quo, free thinkers hell-bent on crushing conservatism.

This sounds romantic doesn't it? It wasn't. While I was in the middle of this rebellion, I never seen myself in this light. We didn't consider ourselves revolutionaries, we were just hooked on becoming innovative advocates for change. We were afraid. We viewed transformation as potentially a very good thing. Being in the middle of that kind of revolution changes you permanently. As artists, we weren't worried whether people, or businesses, or government…or society, would agree with us.

Art had its own purpose — to explore, and to reinvent.

Art is Thinking

In the history of this earth, science, and math have had an integral impact in the biography of humanity. Much of the advancements in medicine, travel, and communication owe their successes to advancements in these fields.

Comparably…art has made it unconceivable to ignore its massive impact on human-kind. Some of us may not recognize it but, art's significance has been with us forever, as far back as history is recorded. I believe it may be part of our spiritual DNA. Just like science and math, art sets us apart as special creatures from all the rest. Unlike math, science, history and commerce — art is chock full of extra special stuff in a number of unique ways.

In the most humble manner I can explain to you, art does stand alone. Art is unique. Here's why.

Let me answer you with this question. Once you've taken a breath, where did it go? Is it gone? It seems magical. Breathing gives life and appears to take nothing back in return. There are many things in life just like this, that are difficult for most of us to explain.

For instance: It seems amazing to me that although the origins of math is visible everywhere in the cosmos, wherever art appears, math seems to disappear. It seems impossible for us to observe both of them at the same time, unless you are Albert Einstein or Leonardo da Vinci.

And yet, people will, at times, overlook an artist or the art as having little tangible economic value. What people need to learn is, art may be described as instinctual and mystical, but it also should be categorized as what it truly is — extremely and intensively written invisible math.

That is correct. Math…by its nature, plans without any regard to humanity, while art…by its unique nature, disrupts the universe in order to serve humanity.

They are so very different, and yet, they depend upon each other to survive.

Art is mysterious, while math is logical and undeniable. Because of this enigma, in general, people tend to trust math, and to distrust art. This is the reason Ansel Adams said he became a photographer, rather than a painter. Photography is seen as technical. As a photographer, he thought, his art would be taken more seriously.

Looking back on this, it may seem to be a sad recount, but the world has benefited from his misjudgment.

The Differences between Math and Art

History has given us many individuals, great thinkers and doers, who've seemed to transcend time. Galileo Galilei, Isaac Newton, Benjamin Franklin, and Albert Einstein were such characters. There are some who place artists Pablo Picasso, Bob Dylan, Andy Warhol, and Edgar Allan Poe among them also.

Contrary to general thought, these mere mortals were not ahead of their time, as we sometimes refer to them. It's just that the rest of us were far behind them.

Let me explain it in this way: If math is a picture, then art is how you feel when you look at it. A mathematician says simple things in a complex way. An artist shows intricate thoughts in a simple way. And yet strangely so, art and math cohabit the same space. The same exact space.

People walk the earth every day zombie-like, going through our repeated motions, but when a certain song comes on, a friend shares a remark, or you observe a sunset exploding in the distance — in that moment your life is changed. You may not notice it, but your face alters as well as the tempo of your breathing. In that very moment, you have been transformed.

There is comparable beauty between math and in science, but artists are unique. An artist will recognize the beauty in a solar system. A mathematician will find it very difficult to see logic in a painting of the universe.

There is a reason they are different. Creative people don't see art as a set of equations, a project or an assignment.

They see it as breathing.

Art is Breathing

You are never promised your next breath, nor your next masterpiece. Creative people understand this statement and because of this, tend to live in the moment.

Steve Jobs explains it in his own way. *"Creativity is just connecting things. When you ask people how they did something, they feel a little guilty because they didn't really do it, they just saw something. It seems obvious to them after a while."*

Famed Russian author Leo Tolstoy once wrote, *"Art is not a pleasure or an amusement; art is a great matter. Just like lungs and a heart, art is an organ of human life, transmitting man's reasonable perceptions into feeling."*

People don't make art, or become artists to become rich or to accomplish long-term financial goals. Art isn't a fascination. They make art because they are inspired to do so. Serial entrepreneurs are equally inspired. Entrepreneurs have the ability to see how undetectable puzzle pieces can potentially fit together. It doesn't appear as work to them al tall. They enjoy searching for mysteries and uncovering their hidden solutions.

Art is Symbiotic to Success

No one can deny the immersive impact that business has, and is, making on society. Humans have been dependent upon the structure that commerce has provided humanity to survive.

Just as in business, art is one of those vital building blocks of civilization. Every culture in every land, and in every time, has embraced the creative mind to explain the complexity of the universe, used it to comfort others, and make very complicated things simpler to imagine or understand. Just as a civilization cannot exist without business, it cannot be tolerated without art. Art breathes life into business. Society that does not value its artistic expressions is a civilization that does not value itself. While true that society could survive without the arts, it would quickly become a tedious and miserable existence.

Comic actor W.C. Fields once said, *"The clever cat eats cheese, then breathes down the rat holes with baited breath."* No business mind could have uttered these words. Only an artist or entrepreneur could've penned this, and then laughed out vigorously afterward.

Neuroscientists have shown us that music and the arts light up our brain cells in a way nothing else can. Unlike any other, art and music is associated with higher cognitive function and an expanded learning potential in humans.

Numerous studies done over the past decade have established many amazing and verifiable benefits of integrating one or more of the arts into all important human endeavors including: education, urban development, engineering, health care, and community planning.

Any corresponding lack of artistic influence on a community causes an almost immediate degradation in community health, municipal growth, core education potentials, and a general sociological, descending malaise. This eventually leads to civic abandonment and eventual social desolation.

But, once artists return to a dying community, new life breathes, and business returns. We've seen instances of these rebirths across America in Detroit MI, Buffalo NY, Oakland CA, Pittsburgh PA, and in cities worldwide.

Art Is Good for Entrepreneurs

Here is a question with an obvious answer. If you have the choice, would you rather thrive or survive? Most would choose to thrive, of course. Survival means to live, by accepting necessary hardships, but to thrive is to grow and develop powerfully and energetically, without inhibitions.

Now…have you ever been in a meeting where the agenda moves so slow, it feels like someone must have either died, or got fired? I have. The atmosphere in the room becomes heavy. People begin by staring at each other, then quickly turn away in hopes that no one will notice them. Time seems to stand still, and the clock on the wall ticks slowly and loudly. No one here is thriving. The mood in that room isn't joy or love, it's survival. A goal-oriented administrator may attempt to shock attendees into attention, but it cannot change the air they're breathing.

The problem isn't that those present in the meeting aren't smart or creative, they may be. They just don't believe it.

"Many highly talented, brilliant, creative people think they're not. The role of a creative leader is not to have all the ideas; it's to create a culture where everyone can have ideas and feel that they're valued."
                                                    - Ken Robinson

Unlike administrators, engineers, and accountants…artists tend to have this self-value thing hardwired into them. I'm not saying that they are self-centered, not at all — quite the opposite. They seem to be selflessly, project centered. To an artist, *self* is not the focus.

Because of this, practically speaking, it would benefit most entrepreneurs to invite a creative to lunch. Artistic expressions can help us to understand ourselves. Using creativity in communication teaches us to respect both the diversity of our community, and the strength of our traditions, using a common non-lingual tongue.

Think about this. Who is more entrepreneurial than an artist? Who is more of an artist than an entrepreneur? Both have new ideas, and meet with resistance to change. Both are driven by inspiration and self-motivated to individual success. Better than half the time, neither know if their future plans are going to succeed. Few of them will actually make a living by selling their art, or their newest invention.

French novelist George Sand wrote, *"The artists vocation is to send light into the heart of man."* Just as artists, the brightest business entrepreneurs are also inspired. Not able to restrain themselves, they are compelled to create something, from nothing. They recognize the important values that human nature embodies.

That is..in order to succeed, you'll need to find a purpose to serve. Once you've found your purpose, you'll have to learn what the true meaning is, to *serve*, or impart value to others.

As an avowed believer in the power that branding wields, I recognize certain things to be true:

> 1. **All** people desire to be valued either singularly, or as part of a group
> 2. **Most** people, if given a choice, prefer the safety of a larger group
> 3. **Some** people will have a preference to stand out from a group, while continuing to be a part of it

In general, people desire the safety of community, while they also crave originality. They prefer retaining the safety of being part of a collective, meanwhile insisting on the separateness of individuality. This set of values is consistently observed and treasured in all cultures, religions, nationalities, and in every historical reference. It is locked in to the way we work, think and live our lives.

Artists ignore these (All-Most-Some) values. I don't mean they fight against it. I mean they'll create new ideas by ignoring them. Genius artistic thinkers like Salvador Dali, Mahatma Gandhi, Muhammad Ali, Albert Einstein, John Lennon, and President Lyndon B. Johnson defied traditions, and gave a fresh perspective to their world mired in values, that at times, imprisoned them.

Seen much like *Perfection* (which is the impossibility we aspire to, *Hope* is seen as pie in the sky thinking. But, to a creative mind, Hope is not a daydream or imaginary apple pie, it is an expectation, a goal — an optimistic faith that absolutely can be achieved by allowing your mind to access the power to create.

This creativity is in all of us. I see it every day. People generally do not believe me, but it is true. It's not that it doesn't exist, it's that people do not see it. They are blind to their own artistic creativity. Much like the story about the six blind men describing an elephant in different ways. People are blind to their own artistic inspiration. Thinking they need to know how to hold a paint brush, a camera, or computer software, they are blind to what it truly means to be an artist.

Art is Inside You too

Artists, scientists, and successful entrepreneurs use this same process. The four steps in creativity are: *Preparation, Incubation, Illumination,* and *Verification*. The best medical surgeon I know, was at one time a student in art. The plumber you call would benefit from these classes also.

This may come as a slight surprise to you that genius theoretical physicists, Albert Einstein and Richard Feynman were artists too. Feynman loved to paint. Einstein played the violin and the piano to help him think clearly. Einstein's wife told how he appeared to be lost in thought and taking notes while playing the piano for quite some time. After a while he emerged from his study with his new theory, general relativity. *"The greatest scientists are artists as well,"* Einstein was quoted to say.

Scientists innovate by standing on the shoulders of giants, and so artists of all types create new things or ideas by allowing the activity of incubation to flourish without disparity, illuminating the process, and their humanity.

Cognitive scientists have discovered that this act, of creating art and music, escalates the brain activity like no other human action. Inspiration provides the impetus for the brain regions to temporarily allow for intercommunication. Creativity floods more areas of the brain with movement between divided regional areas, enabling neurons to, not only communicate to each other, but to achieve a collaborative single goal. The cell barriers have been removed and innovation has begun!

I find it interesting that Ivy League business schools are now inviting artists and musicians to discuss their craft — how they begin work, and how they keep inspired, in hopes that students learn to apply these principles into their studies. What they've found is, unlike conventional business studies, artists maintain the ability to focus on an agenda, meanwhile remaining free to switch gears and explore other potential options at any point in the process.

Since this program's implementation, business school graduates have learned new ways to move the process forward, taking charge while learning to create the coalitions necessary for success. They're learning now how to de-polarize their thinking. New ideas flourish.

Adding the arts to a business school curriculum has been impactful into creating extremely high-potential leaders and entrepreneurs. The reasoning is that when business values community, all of humanity benefits with this experience. Within that new conversation, art is always highlighted, and lauded, as a vital expression of humanity, not merely an act of human expression.

Additionally, in general, artists tend to remain flexible, and can accept change. Their mindset is to explore without becoming fixed to any arbitrary, or specific goals. This allows an artist (or a young business turk) to remain in a positive mindset, despite any unforeseen handicaps.

Creative minds play with the objects they love. Obstacles are regarded as new opportunities to explore.

My paramount point remains. Just as with math or with science…you should never equate art as tangental. It is in fact, elemental.

Whether you are a photographer, an engineer or entrepreneur, art is basic. It is a way to explore. If your business employs creative individuals in any form, it is in your best interest to exploit them and their strange logic to a greater degree. Invite them to planning meetings…and yes, to lunch. Your artsy-fartsy creatives deserve better. And, so do you. Their methodologies may bend your sensibilities, but together you may create a new way to dialog, and thereby come up with solutions to some of your super intensely annoying cans of worms.

Chapter Thirteen

The Hungry and the Foolish

I don't know how you feel about this, but I am a little sad, and just a bit frustrated that people over 50 years of age are, for the most part, passed over in today's workforce. Perhaps I feel this way because I too fall into this group.

Change may be inevitable, I know, but I think we should be able to admit that history has shown us time and again, that not all change has been necessarily good or beneficial. We humans can make big mistakes, and may not even recognize them, until we are reminded in the future. Hindsight is the name for history's older brother.

So, without any reservations, I am going to go out on a thin limb here in saying that, I believe huge mistakes have been made by many hiring managers in the past decade. If you are young, you may not recognize this occurring, or being a real thing, until a family member clues you in.

We have failed to take beneficial advantage of our older generation — for their wisdom, their life experiences, their ability to adapt to change, and their gratefulness. And, because of this, our American workforce vibrancy will unquestionably be suffering for a very long time.

You may be *one of the fallen* and have been personally impacted by this phenomenon. If you are, and I am correct on this, then you are probably already way ahead of me on this. To those of you who have not been impacted yet, you'd better prepare for a rough ride in the future. Please read on.

As time continues, it has become increasingly difficult for baby-boomers and retirees to land meaningful, relevant employment. Like it or not, this proclivity companies have towards employing youth seems to have become the new prime directive in hiring. In today's business climate, the radiance of youth seems to carry more contextual weight than years of experience and a lifetime of achievements.

Interestingly, to me, the proliferation and wide corporate adoption of this trend is based upon a morsel of reasoning and truth. And so, we should look at this.

It's Never Too Late

It is often said that younger employees may be more in touch with Generation-X, Y & Z habits, and local crowd trends, which we all know are growing market areas. They also are likely to work for less annually and solicit less financial maintenance than the older generation. Young people will tolerate longer work hours and can be easier to train. These are all good reasonings. But the main supposition hiring managers rely upon with this *prime directive*, is the unqualified notion (that we cannot actually measure), young people have more revolutionary and original ideas, compared with older employees.

I'm not going to argue against this point because, in many cases this may actually be true. In all honesty, I do suggest to you that I believe these enlistment decisions are largely fortified by financial motivations, and not because of best hiring practices. On this, we do have data.

Let's begin by agreeing on this one thing. We know that the very best lies we've ever fallen for, have been generously basted with truth. This is what makes the untruth compelling to begin with. These deceptions are most likely to be based upon truths that we already know. This is how we can be fooled by them. Let's try not to give in to this though, without at least a quick examination.

Most major commitments in life are deeply rooted in economics. When you get married, purchase a car, choose a roommate, relocate your home, or accept a new job offering…these are all good examples. It is usually because it is financially an optimum time to make these life changes. *"Money changes everything,"* Cyndi Lauper used to sing. It is not just a title to a once popular song, she's right.

Although we may be able to justify these new recruitment methods fiscally, time has shown us that involuntary, knee-jerk judgement calls, like this, are greatly lacking in some very important, indispensable and foundational areas. In order to remain viable and robust to investors, hiring departments who make the decision to go down this rabbit hole, will be required to cover themselves for these choices by using two adoptive maneuvers:

1) They will need to find a way to justify these methods, *and*
2) A replacement will have to be created for what conceptually will be lost

Unexpectedly, and quite accidentally, they were able to achieve both of these demands. True to the times, they've found an App for it, that solved both of these problems.

Birth of the App Age

The business world gave birth to the App Age. There are apps for computers, tablets and phones. Apps that are embedded within games, on televisions, in your car dashboard, and even at your restaurant table. In this era of applications, we're constantly looking for an App to do some task for us. We rarely do things in time-honored, slow and steady, ways. Since we don't need to remember things or write them down any longer, an App on a device can do that for us. Connecting the invisible dots between important bits of information in our daily lives is no longer a personal art, but by using an App, we now call it *science*. In this new era, experience plays a very minimal part. Artificial intelligence (AI) and machine learning is business's new wonder drug of choice. There's an App for everything, and if there isn't, let's just create one we need.

Everything is data. Data is everything. Doo-dah!, doo-dah! (please forgive my sarcasm).

Leading smart-marketing, AI proponent companies such as *Marketo®*, *SharpSpring®*, and *HubSpot®*, (there are a vast multitude more of them), boast about business success being attainable by supplying and training marketers in utilizing marketing automation applications. Google®, Facebook®, Twitter®, and others do this too. These companies make millions of dollars by convincing business customers into thinking that they can always trust data. Their apps track, compile, sort, and delineate who the customer is, and predict what they might do next. These are very important and potentially powerful tools, in the right hands. I say, *"in the right hands,"* because information of itself, is completely useless in the wrong hands.

Allow me to sidetrack you for just a moment. I'll come back to this topic later.

Let's take up the topic of *Youth* for a bit. Years of case studies have shown that our current generation is more savvy than previous eras. No matter what you read in the blogs about the failures of schools today, this generation of kids are required to do more classwork than you did in your day. In addition, honed by years of internet search, social surfing, and video gaming, their impulse reaction time is far superior to yours or mine. They can stay up half the night, long after I'm already in bed. They multi-task without trying. Their eyes are better than mine too. I concede all of these as truths.

Most sixteen or seventeen year olds cannot wait to learn to drive. Using the above case study data and our combined personal experience, this hiring *prime directive* concept tells us that it should be to the benefit for all of us, to be enlisting and trusting our generation of youth to drive our heavy haulers, mega fork lifts, nuclear submarines, and oil tankers.

High-risk transports such as these demand the highest dexterity, talent, speed, and skill to pilot them. OK?

Why then, do decades of driving statistics tell us that younger drivers cause three times the vehicle accidents of mature drivers? What happened to the data in this case? Maybe there is more to data, than the objective digits.

If you've ever driven on the road in a hard Texas rain, or in the Minnesota snow at night, or in a busy California intersection right after a large elementary school has let their kids out…you're going to be in a situation you just cannot handle. Even the sharpest of us can fray.

People forget that there are things far more important than data — or reaction time, or youth. It is one thing to have skill, or even knowledge, and quite another to be able to measure and compare current facts with historical insights, filtered by a time-sharpened intuition. It may seem like an odd thing to say, but, every so often, math by itself, can lead you astray. Sometimes 1 + 3 will equal 5.

All of the figures and statistics within an App or a spreadsheet, won't help you to know that until it's too late to make a needed adjustment.

HISTORICAL EXAMPLE

The vast majority of distinguished historical trailblazers had never achieved greatness during their youth. In fact, quite a number of them peaked long past their prime.

Yesterdays pioneers, Henry Ford, Jonas Salk, Thomas Edison, Wilber and Orville Wright, all were close to forty years of age, before they achieved any form of success or recognition. Noah Webster, J.R.R. Tolkien, and Cornelius Vanderbilt were over sixty years, before their success.

Within this generation, our groundbreaking geriatric innovators were KFCs Harland Sanders, Comedian

Rodney Dangerfield, Martha Stewart, Vera Wang, Duncan Hines, and Marvel's Stan Lee.

Sometimes it can take time for a genius to gel.

"The best thing about getting older is knowing history. The longer you live, the more you know, and the more you know, you will see where things started." - John Madden

Our generation had Steve Jobs, who died way before his time. This is still painful for me to recall. It's not because he past on at the early age of fifty-six. It was in what the world had lost, and would have continued to be captivated and amazed by today, should he had lived in health just two more decades.

What is my point? My point is we are expecting way too much from our youth and in our piles of data. Mistakes are bound to happen. It's not fair them, and the rest of us in society either. We should be able to utilize history to our advantage. Because, in general we do not, here is what has, and will, continue to happen…

Companies that follow this habit of hiring young brilliant minds, will have to rely deeply upon these super data mining applications to be perfect in their delineations, exact in their predictions…and, able to leap tall buildings in a single bound. The future fate of companies will be completely in virtual hands. Having no experience to lean on, our new young experts on which we will depend, will also have to be magnificent coders and insightful guessers.

This is what grinds on me. I feel bad for them, because no single person can be this good. I hope it troubles you too, at least a little. These self-collating Apps will have to make up for experience and instinct — and they just can't.

They may be able to do marvelous things, but a robot will never be equal to out-paint Picasso, or connect with customers' future purchasing habits like Steve Jobs. Never.

At a Stanford University commencement speech in 2005, Steve Jobs told the young crowd of graduates, *"Stay hungry. Stay Foolish."* Although he was actually quoting from *The Whole Earth Catalog*, most people attending thought he meant that, the age of youth being savagely impressionable, is preferable to adulthood, or that being young and reckless may be one of the fundamentals to success.

You'd be wrong in both cases, but don't feel bad. People often misunderstood Steve.

A reporter once asked artist Pablo Picasso how he stayed so youthful. He responded with a glare, a grin, and a simple *"Youth has no age"* rebuke. You've probably heard this phrase more than a few times before.

Why This is Branding Truth

Authoritative power brands clearly understand the large influence that diversity imparts, and they protect it as a valuable resource. Once you reduce your thinking (or hiring focus) to age or gender, race or region, PhD or GED , physical appearance or discernible defect, you'll limit your possibilities and the eventual success of your company, or project. Likewise, when you do hire, smarter is generally better — but not necessarily younger.

The fact is…we will always need each other. Surely, we can be hungry or foolish at any age. We can even become mathematicians and artists…at the same time! We can be young and wise, or old and brave. I believe it. But, in order for you to see it too, first you'll have to learn to simply accept this as a possibility, and then let go.

Learn to Let Go

I can sympathize with those who dislike change. I'm not a huge fan of it either. Learning to accept adjustments are disconcerting. We hate the thought that we might be going backwards and reliving some part of our ugly past.

But, change is inevitable. We know that too. Learning to let go and to adapt, will be key to success.

Here's how I see it. I consider every day as birth, and every tomorrow as re-birth. The past has not changed, but you have. You should remember this too, because once you do forget, your eternal youth spirit will also begin to die. You will have become so enamored with your destination, you will have forgotten to enjoy the incredibly fascinating journey that your life is on. On that tragic day, you will begin to grow old. You will become polarized, switching sides without even becoming aware of it. Logic will supersede Creativity. The two once stalwart allies, will no longer live and work together, as they were originally intended. Life will change without us knowing. Deceiving ourselves into concluding that we have not changed, but we have only matured, we will end up working harder, misleading ourselves into believing that we are smarter.

Should we regain some composure, it may already be too late for us to let go. We will unconsciously have become polarized, losing the innate ability to collaborate and connect with each other in a real, honest, and incredibly fascinating way.

Chapter Fourteen

Why You Should Hire a Monkey

Familiar images come to mind when we think of monkeys. They are seen as being cute, precocious and hilariously funny, tree-swinging creatures, of which they assuredly are. They are known for getting into mischief no matter their environment. Humans love to watch them. Because people have this conception, primates are generally viewed as the ingenious comedians of the animal kingdom. Yes, monkeys are viewed as clowns, wisecrackers and court jesters of the animal kingdom. I don't ever remember hearing them being referred to as experts at social dissemination, motivational speaking, or market research gravitas. This would be considered shockingly silly.

But, times have changed and so has our thinking. After generations of research, we have learned a few new things about primates. Boy…it appears that we have been so terribly wrong, in every way, about them. In fact, we've learned so much about monkeys in this last decade alone, it has surprised even the experts, so I'm thinking it should both amaze and captivate you, too.

Studied intensely for decades by biologists, zoologists, and archeologists, we are becoming amazingly better informed. Our simian siblings have so much more to offer, and teach us, than we had ever realized. Often compared with less cerebral creatures of the forest glade, monkeys and apes are now finally earning their due respect as the true intellects of the animal kingdom.

You may be surprised at what I share next.

Movies such as *Rise of the Planet of the Apes,* and *Project X,* may have somewhat tweaked our views of the cerebral capability in monkeys, showing them to potentially occupy a higher intelligence than we might have originally dreamed, but these flicks have only scratched the surface to their cognizance potential. They leave out some very important neural nuances that monkeys possess. These movie scripts may illustrate a fresh balance for us in brains vs. brawn, but this is all. This isn't any more surprising than watching a cat who raises ducklings, or a police officer playing basketball with street kids. Real life can be very surprising to us — we get that. We've seen the weirdest interactions and fantasies on TV and Youtube.

But, this is not what I'm talking about. We know a great deal about monkeys, and yet, there is still much we don't understand. Monkeys possess an unsurpassed uniqueness that movies, television, or the internet has yet to capture.

Monkeys Know How to Thrive

For instance, unlike many animals, monkeys seem to be able to do wonderfully well in captivity. Not just adaptable, compliant or resilient…they flourish, even in the absence of freedom. This may not seem to you to be a big deal. It is. As extremely intelligent creatures, primates seem to thrive at accommodating in some of the worst stressful environments the world has to offer. Way better than any known sentient animal, even human beings.

This means something.

We've all seen videos of monkeys going *bananas*. It's funny to watch them romp around in chaotic dismay. When we humans watch this, we attribute their actions as being, *unplugged*. Although extreme turmoil appears to strain their ability to reason, we now know that they have, in fact, not detonated or imploded as their physical appearance infers. Surprisingly, they are still under full control, although visually it looks quite the exact opposite.

Here's what analysis has concluded. Monkeys are not in panic mode as they appear to be in — they have simply just shifted into a second gear. They're still plugged in, but into a different source.

They see agitation as an opportunity. They willingly adjust in order to survive together. Humans make these type of adjustments to their lifestyle only under extreme pressure.

Better at adapting than humans, primates show all of the positive psychological markers of being masters at transforming negative situations into positive ones — at turning lemons into lemonade.

Monkeys Make Fantastic Communicators

Being superb care-givers and excellent communicators, primates have a wide range of collaborative abilities they employ to keep in constant contact with their community, their soul mates, their at-risk young and old, and even their enemies. They utilize a variety of complex verbal and visual pitches, to call a mate, to announce where there is food in the area, to warn of danger, and to communicate and to train and educate, their less fortunate and young.

Like their human counterparts, monkeys are known to both create and use tools that help them in adapting to any situation. But, unlike some animals, they can show a wide variety of emotions: love, anger, sadness, mourn the loss of loved ones, and even smile and laugh at the appropriate moment. They are experts at emoting sadness or happiness. When they determine a certain situation is entertaining, they'll find the right spot and set the stage, sharing the amusing anecdote to others. They teach and reprimand. They will persuade others to peace, or warn others of oncoming war. They can share or steal, if required. Monkeys seem to have this special knack for knowing the perfect time to console, or to share levity. They have perfect timing.

Monkeys Recognize Their Faults

Unlike us humans, monkeys never lose sight of who they are. They love community and abhor abandoning others. They have a healthy sense of self, and yet they crave community. They take good care of their young, old and defenseless. They love communicating in a fun and safe, supportive environment — connecting with community. Monkeys nearly always prefer a win-win scenario.

They understand that when all involved benefit from peace, individuality, profitability and peace abound.

Monkeys make perfect, loyal partners who aren't afraid to show their fun side either. They know that humor is a very effective communication tool. Fun creatures are amusing and keep boredom to a minimum. Creative levity relieves social stress and corporate tension. It can increase trust and bonding between individuals. Humor is also vital to message building.

- Adapting to succeed
- Communicating in compassionate ways
- Staying true to self
- Not taking yourself too seriously

These are important traits to desire, don't you think?

If you've been reading and following, I think you'll agree with me that these attributes would make perfect brand partners and a reliable and desirable workforce.

And so, if you're looking to hire or promote… if you desire to find loyal, dedicated, and harmonic colleagues… ones who will stop at nothing to find creative ways to collaborate and build a super-connected and high-spirited community.

As you begin your search for team builders, please remember the most important premise I am purporting in this chapter. Do yourself, your company, and your customers a magnanimous and enlightened favor.

Hire a monkey.

Chapter Fifteen

Stay Thirsty My Friends

If you have been faithful to reading this entire volume, I appreciate your dedication and interest in this subject that I love to write about. Hopefully you've been enlightened or at least entertained. You've probably also learned that besides being a writer and enthusiastic disciple in inspirational branding…I am also a lifelong creative.

I love every variety of personal artistic expression — painting and drawing, printmaking and sculpture, cell animation, video and photography, both fine art and commercial design. I love them all, and have made at least modest attempts at most of them in my life.

And, despite having worked in the advertising and branding industry for nearly three decades, I continue to love viewing television commercials too. You wouldn't think I could enjoy watching them at all, after being placed at the epicenter of this creative chaos for such a long period, but believe it or not, I'm still fascinated by them. I find that commercials can be, at times, the most entertaining part of watching television. For me, broadcast advertising can also be a powerful and super fun way to communicate monumental, and lasting messages.

I find that product ads that contain humor are the most fun for me to watch, and can be the most memorable. Most of us love to laugh, at ourselves and others, too. Their has been many attempts throughout history to entice us to try, or to lure us to look, using humor.

Then, there are those ads created and placed in order to serve society in some way. Social commentary or health related. They provide a very important public purpose.

My favorite ones though, are those thirty-second miracles that surreptitiously work their magic, inspiring you and I to be the very best versions of ourselves, changing not only how we think, but how we live our lives.

Peruvian department store, *Saga Falabella*, hit one out of the park with their 2006 *"Dare"* TV ad. Have you seen it? What a remarkably inspiring piece of social inspiration. Using Vivaldi's spectacular music, *Summer*, as a backdrop, it dares women to persistently challenge themselves.

Most of us can recall Nike®'s *"Just Do It"* campaign. This iconic commercial has been able to sprint well past its intended short run, into a brand phenom mantra for sports enthusiasts worldwide. This theme encourages even the least of us, to accomplish our ultimate best.

Coca-Cola® produced the hope filled, "I'*d like to buy the world a Coke,*" commercial in 1971. This was at a perfect time for America, who had grown exhausted and drained by the length of the Vietnam war. Its message was clear. Peace and harmony is always preferable to war. Along with the Apple® ad, "*1984*", these are possibly the most powerful and memorable of all television ads in our time.

In 2018, InfinityUSA® created a commercial with an interesting angle. In it's "The Rules of Luxury" ad, they make an interesting effort to validate the guilt-free enjoyment of opulence, through negative messaging. "*Look, but don't touch; Touch, but don't use; Use, but don't enjoy; Enjoy, but don't show it. Luxury should be lived in,*" they claim. Don't be like those other people. Go ahead and enjoy!

There are many interesting and inspiring ad spots that I could share, but there is one that stands out for very specific reasons, and I'd really love to share it with you.

The Dos Equis® beer commercial has been around for well over a decade. It always ends with *the most interesting man in the world* saying, *"Stay thirsty my friends"*.
It's written in a way to induce you to an agreeable chuckle. Among all of the many commercials that I am fond of, this one created by Euro RSCG Worldwide is definitely on my top five or ten list, primarily because, although it may be fantastically amusing, it is also one that offers the viewer genuine encouragement. It advocates that you have undisputed possibilities and a very bright future — that you are smarter, stronger, and better than you believe. It touches on a very basic human truth — that our purpose in living on this earth is to enjoy life, all the delights of being human, and to share them with others.

Down deep, we all know this truth to have merit, but how many of us actually believe that this brand of hope and inspiration, actually includes us?

As a former copywriter required to count his words, I carefully watched this commercial one day a few times. I began to scrutinize the phrase, *"Stay thirsty my friends"*. It is a very interesting choice of words, isn't it? In this commercial, the protagonist doesn't ask us to be thirsty, or to get thirsty, but he engages us to *stay thirsty*. So, what does that actually mean…to stay thirsty? It is a very peculiar phrase. Although we can rationalize that this may be just a fun metaphoric phrase meant to stimulate us into grabbing all the gusto (and beer) we can, I believe it has a much more profound significance than we might first realize. We should take a few moments to comprehend the full meaning that may have been originally intended.

Boxing legend George Foreman once confessed to a reporter, *"As a child, I was so terribly hungry that I used to dream that one day I'd get locked up all night in a grocery store."* I have experienced what it feels like to be a little hungry, but I've never been that kind of hungry before. While I've known what hunger can feel like, I have absolutely no idea at all what it means, to stay hungry, absolutely in need of food.

We have all heard, and/or seen, health-minded people go on hunger fasts, cleansing their bodies, by giving up on certain foods or drink, or subsisting solely on only one type of food for a period. The goal in doing so is to either clear the mind, refresh the body, to lose some excess weight, or to make a political or religious statement.

History has many examples. Here are two.

In the fall of 1924, preeminent leader of the Indian independence movement, Mahatma Gandhi, went on a self-imposed three-week hunger strike in an attempt to encourage two religious parties to reconcile. Before his assassination in 1948, he used this hunger form of protest a total of at least seventeen times.

At the turn of this century, an American suffragette by the name of Alice Paul, refused to eat anything at all, after being imprisoned for protesting on behalf of the rights of women. Her prison guards had to force-feed her raw eggs through a tube, just so that she would not die in jail.

Throughout history, hunger has often been used as the centerpiece of a message — a sociopolitical tool that bureaucratic committees, well-meaning individuals, or faith-based groups could leverage like a political football to push their political agenda, their products, or message.

In cases such as these, hunger is generally used more as a militant *motivational* tool, than it is an *inspirational* spark.

Let me explain myself.

No person *desires* to be hungry. This fact may be obvious. We love to eat. Some of us plan our existences around what to eat, when we eat, and where. Many of our life events (birthdays, weddings, holidays, spiritual gatherings, school graduations, movie nights, wedding and baby celebrations) have some type of special food formally presented. Unlike the others in the animal kingdom who eat to live, food is a big deal for humans. We live to eat.

So, when one of us makes a commitment to NOT eat, it is a really big deal. Some of us may beg the question…why? It can give us peculiar and unnatural feelings, forcing us to challenge the intention behind this decision. We know that people, as a matter of course, can and do make choices such as these. We also understand that when they do, they do so because, either they have been forced to, or there is an issue they are attempting to change or correct.

To those of you who may be willing to agree with me... I see Fasting and Hunger as very different convictions.

Are You Hungry, or Are You Fasting?

Hunger focuses on an acute physical need, while fasting is nearly always linked with an inspired, or spiritual desire.

Hunger is usually exploited or motivated by an external force on a person or group, by anther person or group. In general, we can also define **motivation** as an outside force pushing in, or on us, despite our pleas for respite. Guilt, coercion, sin and/or duty are huge influences.

Fasting, on the other hand, is driven by self, through an unselfish, and yet passionate, internal transformation. This self-propelled force by an inward influence is what we sometimes refer to as **inspiration**. When inspired, we won't require guilt, a person, or a social influence, any outside impetus at all, to vigorously direct our obligations. There is no pressure of any type on us, that we have not already formulated for ourselves. We appear as free.
And so, if we are the slightest bit confused by this, we should ask ourselves this very important question; Are we motivated by hunger or are we inspired by it?

Unlike simply going hungry, fasting seems to be hard-wired to deep thought, prayer, or meditation. Contrary to hunger, fasting is always an incorporeal, strictly personal decision. Without this form of reflection, fasting isn't complete; it is simply going hungry with a purpose.

Although very few of us can say we've lived a life as rich as *'the most interesting man in the world,'* the majority of us do consider ourselves blessed. Many of us in the U.S. eat two to three meals each day. As far back in time as we can recall, eating was (and still is) an everyday part of our human existence. We tend to eat, not because we are necessarily hungry, but generally because — it is just time to eat. When we do go a little bit hungry, it is either purely by mischance, or because of some unscheduled time constraint. In either case, down deep, we are well aware that we've broken our consistent daily conclave with our oral pleasure, and it simply feels odd to be hungry.

When we opt to make this strange change in our schedule, by purposefully abstaining from our daily eating ritual, we realize that there has been an odd disruption in the normal rhythm of our life. In our voluntarily refuse of pleasure (as in fasting), we are voluntarily admitting that we understand that something in 'the force' is wrong — for we were created to enjoy, not to suffer. When we become self-aware, when we recognize this, it behooves us to make a change, and re-align with new goals. This is fasting — choosing to stay hungry. The men and women who make this decision, do so because they realize that something very bad may have occurred, but something else better is also coming. In this way staying hungry, or fasting, can take on a twofold significance, right along with grieving and hope. When we fast we're admitting that we feel the need to take a giant step backward, in order to perceive a radically different future for ourselves.

Throughout history, and in every culture, this ritual has been consistently linked in conjunction with themes of disruption and/or restoration. Hunger may be forced upon us, while fasting is an entirely personal issue.

Three hundred years ago french writer Voltaire wrote, *"With great power comes great responsibility."* Ha! I'll bet you thought Stan Lee wrote that. Our countries founders would have agreed with this thought. This freedom that we love, comes with conditions. This liberty that we enjoy, actually suggests that our freedom to choose, is not just a freedom to benefit. Our choosing to do, or not do, can have serious ramifications. Our choice to decide, is the foundation of living a fruitful life. We are not forced, we have a very critical contribution — choice. Our liberty is linked directly to our freedom to choose.

How does this freedom to opt-in or out relate to fasting? Why is *'staying thirsty'* important?

One way to think about this might be that, just because something is within our reach, does not mean that it is also our license to selfishly enjoy. Fasting is primarily an act of willing abstinence or reduction from certain or all food, drink, or pleasure, for a specified period of time. But, if you consider it fasting, it has a greater purpose than self.

Hunger is Always Connected to Something

Further scrutiny should convince you that this is actually more of a principle, than it is a particular personal action.

Staying hungry, or fasting, does not mean you are ever hungry in the physical sense. It must have an internal motive, with conditions and timing being critical factors.

Those who *fast*, do so for a completely different purpose than filling some uncomplicated desire to be indulged. Meanwhile, a hungry person can, at times, find it very difficult to comprehend what it is to be wholly satisfied.

To me, this is a fascinating observation about hunger. That is…you may not realize true hunger or thirst, until you first know what it means to be satisfied, or filled up. You cannot merely give a starving person a snack, then tell them they are no longer hungry, even though it may be more food than they've had in weeks. A person who has been confined to a wheelchair from an early age is unlikely to understand what is to run a marathon. If you've never been filled, how can you know what it feels like? You can't hunger for something that you haven't at one time experienced. Only when you've have tasted what you desire, can you comprehend the overwhelming power and weakness of yearning for what you have once tasted.

Where am I going with this? I'm coming to it.

There are those of us who regularly give back. We do wonderful things with our time and money, but in all of our unselfish giving, most of the time we still have plenty left. With all of our sacrifices, we're not experiencing hunger. We haven't been emptied. We don't feel the pain of hunger because we haven't known what empty feels like yet. Finding ourselves between this metaphysical *rock and a squishy place*, we're actually trapped in limbo between giving and getting. We're neither hungry nor filled, and this is a great dilemma that can prevent us from feeling what it means to be inspired.

Stay Hungry, My Friends

Let's go back to that Dos Equis commercial that I admire.

When *the most important man in the world* instructs us to *"Stay thirsty, my friends,"* he's encouraging us to be filled, to take pleasure in living and enjoying it all. No guilt. To enjoy life! But wait, there is more. Immediately following, or better yet, simultaneous to our self gratification, we're not to keep any part of it selfishly, but, after having enjoyed it, we are to share it with others… especially to those we consider as friends.

Humanitarian and religious groups have long observed this same call to sacrifice and service. During the year, when many of us celebrate one of our special days, it is important to remember the vital lesson that this scripted television personality is nebulously sharing with us. Once you begin to savor life, a pivotal change should take place. First you must fill up — then, you must share. Your initial goal should be to take it all in. Enjoy both the cookies and the crumbs in your life, so that you will have a story to tell, and something very valuable to share with others.

To those of us who work in the advertising, marketing, or branding (promotional) space: Please realize that this should be our ultimate objective too. To fill up your customers completely! To be their greatest advocate to enjoying life! To enable them to see their unique potential in the world — one with infinite possibilities to share.

Once your customers sense that you consider them to be *the most interesting persons in the world* (not *your* world, or *their* world, but THE world), they will become changed.

No longer will they glare at their insubstantial, repetitive, and uneventful lives that they observe daily through dark colored glasses. You will have enlightened them. Their vision will become inspired, not motivated. You will be their newly treasured friend, for which they will be inclined to share their personal and amazing journey.

Once they become loyal, devoted to contributing, they will also become filled with an entirely novel capability — the capacity to sacrifice. A significant change has occurred. Upon observing this positive and transformational change in themselves… you, your company, staff and products will become their latest crusade, enriching their own lives, and those whom they regularly engage.

This is not a momentary passing phase. This is a radical revolutionary change that has just occurred. One where enjoyment has a functional purpose far beyond simple pleasure or appetite. Those who are the most gifted at receiving will be the very ones who are most capable of promoting with all confidence, how their life had been changed by your belief in them, and by the fanatical importance of understanding what is means to stay thirsty.

About the Author

Randy Zeyen is a Brand Evangelist, author and speaker living in the San Francisco bay area of California.

For well over three decades, he has found it a great privilege to be an integral part of the American work force innovation, contributing and guiding a number of dynamic, electrified and connected world brands.

Although RandyZ has long been recognized as an award-winning multidisciplinary veteran, a creative brand strategist, tactical designer, coach and mentor…he is also very passionate about writing and speaking on a variety of other topics, including, business connectivity, work/life balance, and the vital significance that diversity plays in the American work space.